THE
WORLD
OF THE
AFRICAN
WOMAN

John E. Eberegbulam Njoku

The Scarecrow Press, Inc.
Metuchen, N.J., & London
1980

Library of Congress Cataloging in Publication Data

Njoku, John E. Eberegbulam.
   The world of the African woman.

   1. Women--Africa. 2. Rural women--Africa.
3. Women in rural development--Africa. 4. Social
change. I. Title.
HQ1788.N56   305.4'2'096   80-23832
ISBN 0-8108-1350-5

To my beloved
mother, Bessie

TABLE OF CONTENTS

THE WORLD OF THE
AFRICAN WOMAN

Chapter 1

INTRODUCTION

Since the beginning of the twentieth century African women
have been active in the development of their rural areas.
One thing common to the African woman, whether she is educated, illiterate, Moslem or Christian, patrilineal or matri-
lineal, in a monogamous or polygamous relationship, is her
responsibility to her family and rural development; however,
it is certain that the role of women in rural economies remains static. "An adequate conception of rural development
in Africa today must consider that rural farm families--men,
women, and children--do not experience rural change in a
uniform manner. Development programs must reflect this
awareness and gauge how development is affecting farm families on the ground."[1]

The Hoe Culture is still the major method used by
African women in the rural farming process. This method
is similar to that used in ancient Egypt and Mesopotamia--a
Y-shaped stick sometimes hardened with bronze. In most
African countries agriculture is still of this hoe-type, unaided

3

by nonhuman power, as animal power is not in use in most African countries today. The plough itself, which made its appearance thousands of years ago in the Nile Valley, has only recently been introduced in some parts of Africa. Therefore most of the farm labor is done by women. Even with the United Nations policy of agricultural extension and the indigenous-countries policy the contacts with farm women have often been negative. Most extension-service teams are composed of men, and these men tend to contact targets who are usually men. Boserup summarizes his study based on colonial agricultural extension policies:

> As a result of the attitude of the Extension services, the gap between the Labour productivity of men and women thus continued to widen. Men are thought to apply modern methods in the cultivation of a given crop, while women continue to use traditional methods in the cultivation of the same crop, thus getting much less out of their efforts than men. The inevitable result is that women are discouraged from participating in agriculture and are glad to abandon cultivation whenever their husband's income makes it possible. [2]

African women are mainly peasant farmers, whose livelihoods depend on the cultivation of subsistence agriculture, although a few of them raise some fowl at home. Men and boys generally tend goats and cattle, with men being responsible for trading cattle and repairing homes and fences. "But the vast majority of African women on the Continent, about 85% of the people, are engaged in subsistence agriculture, faced with lives of hard work."[3]

A series of hardships has made African women very strong physically. They lift and carry on their heads baskets of cassava, yams, bags of garri (tapioca), and Koko yams to the market places for sale. This is virtually the only way they can produce money in the peasant economy. While the women from the Western world and a few educated African women are pushing for equality, the majority of these peasant women are crying out for economic liberation. Their lives of relative poverty do not mean that these women are completely weak; on the contrary, most are strong, healthy individuals who are responsible for the day-to-day feeding of the household. Many women exert a strong influence over men and bring their sanctions of female ancestral spirits to bear upon them. They sometimes resort to strikes, ridicule, and

cursing if they have no formal means of gaining their
ends.

Most of the rural areas are now changing, and this
has had a tremendous impact on African women. They are
witnessing the development of urban settings, which are now
increasingly being drawn into the market economy. Women
in Africa tend to perform dual functions--they are partly
traders and partly farmers. They are involved in supple-
mentarity and complementarity of enterprises. This means
that no African woman has only one activity. She must often
complement a major enterprise, either with food crops or
petty trading. She must have a few acres of land for food
crops around the village and compound. An African woman
does not usually buy all her family's food. She has her vegetable stand around the house, year in, year out, which is
valued as a source of food during periods of emergency. For
instance, during a heavy rainfall, when no one is able to go
to the market or to the farm, food cultivated around the house
is utilized to great advantage. Gulliver states with greater
certainty that Jie women as wives, mothers, and daughters
were equal to men in the household economy because of their
significance in agriculture. "The garden was the woman's
livestock. She cultivated and owned 9/10 of the garden lands.
A woman's economic responsibilities in her yard consisted of
preparing milk products, performing the domestic chores re-
lating to feeding the family and rearing the children."[4] Those
who farm a few areas of land take the commodities to the
village or central market to sell.

"I am suggesting that the problems facing African
women today, irrespective of their national and social class
affiliations, are inextricably bound in the wider struggle by
African people to free themselves from poverty and ideological domination in both intra- and international spheres."[5]
Research has found that the economic position of African
women is better now than it was in precolonial or colonial
times. But the strength of their political organization was
stronger in the colonial period than it is now--history will
always remember the part played by the women from Guinea-
Bissau and Mozambique in African independence.

> Those African societies which have gone through
> great upheavals in the course of anti-colonial strug-
> gles have revealed a deep groundswell of discontent
> among women about the status of women. One saw
> and heard of this repeatedly in Guinea-Bissau during

the long war of liberation fought by the P. A. I. G. C.
against the Portuguese colonial system. A very
large number of women took part in one way or
another, not as women under arms (though there
were some of those too), but as persons upon whom
new responsibilities were thrust whether for the
management of local affairs, the staffing of huge
clinics or elementary schools. 6

The widespread riots of women in southern Nigeria in
1929 will long stand as evidence of the roles of strength, unity,
and determination that African women can play. A riot that
started in Aba, involving mainly the Igbo women from the
eastern part of the country, is an example of women in African political life during the colonial era. "In 1926 the
British in colonial Nigeria undertook a population census as
the first step in imposing a head tax on adult males. In
1929, a chief under instructions from a district officer took
a count of women, children and domestic animals. The chiefs
and Europeans were attacked and properties destroyed. "7

Women's organizations have become important in African countries, increasingly playing a part in everyday life.
Regularly women hold conferences at which they discuss their
unique problems in the development of society. "Not long
ago, in Maputo, capital of Mozambique, the organization of
Mozambican women held such a conference, attended by some
200 women delegates from local branches. Many of them
were illiterate, but all the women were especially subject
to infections 'within the organizations of Mozambican women. ' "8

In many African countries women have often resisted
any situation whenever they felt it would undermine their
womanhood. In the case of southern Nigeria in 1929 the taxation of women violated the basic principles and mores of
Igbo society. However, all these movements have stimulated
their search for liberation and identity. The mishandling of
Nigerian women's resistance in 1929 revealed the weakness
of the colonial administration in that era. The administrators acted as agents of change for a culture they did not
understand. They introduced a tax system as though they
were administering the local government in their mother country. They did not want an explanation of why women could
not accept the imposition of a levy. The philosophy behind
the owing of a debt has some impact on the lives of the people in rural Africa: one has to weigh one's ability to pay.
The idea of owing heavy amounts is discouraged in African

societies. Despite the use of money lenders in the rural
areas the debt collector is much dreaded. In traditional rural Africa debts are normally collected early in the morning.
The debt collector knocks at the debtor's door requesting the
payment of the money usually with 100 percent interest. Because of the pressure from the creditors debt is not a good
thing to mention early in the morning, as it is supposed to
bring bad luck during the day's normal activities.

The market women in Africa are the women who fill
the market--day in, day out--in pursuit of trade. They are
the legendary women who handle most of the retail trade.
Most of the political powers of the African women are derived
from their market organizations. From Nigeria to Senegal
in West Africa, from Ethiopia to Zaire, and from Angola to
Mozambique, women have come together in their market organizations.

> The modern money economy and the needs of new
> nations have opened up new opportunities for women
> to participate in the family decisions and national
> progress. The increasing power of women in the
> consumer market comes from their economic role
> as traders or workers in the modern sector. [9]

> Among Yoruba women migrants, for example, wo-
> men traders usually equal or outnumber male tra-
> ders in terms of absolute numbers and in terms
> of percentage of their respective working popula-
> tions. In Ghana in 1960, Yoruba women traders
> outnumbered their male counterparts by over 2,000.
> They also constitute a relatively greater proportion
> of the female working population than did male tra-
> ders within the working male population. [10]

African women have their personal rights, which include the right to own personal property, such as a farm or
a piece of land, the right to farm the husband's plot, and the
absolute right to buy and sell in the marketplace. However,
with all these rights the African woman still regards herself
as absolutely dependent upon and subordinate to her husband,
the head of the household. To her the marketplace is not
only a place to exchange commodities, but a place to gossip,
criticize friends, show her beautiful charms, her wealth, advertise her title, and to organize the women's clubs. All
her market activities are performed with the permission of
her husband. Whatever profits she realizes after the day's
market activities are often shared with her husband and children.

In her article "Returning to the Gold" Tamar Golan said: "The traditional markets (in Africa) have always been a major feature of life in Africa: marriages are not contracted in traditional markets; marriages could be publicized in the traditional markets of some African societies as a part of the ceremonial features of marriage celebrations. "[11]

Most marriages are contracted according to native laws and customs. Even if one is to have a Christian marriage one first has to complete the necessary procedures according to the traditional laws. It is usually customary for a man, before he takes a woman, to give a bride price to the girl's family. The courtship is by African tradition; not like the Western type of courtship, where a man takes a girl on dates. Rather the girl is invited to the fiance's home for the family to see and scrutinize. The girl has to stay a few days before she goes back to her home. She is tested for many qualities--character, devotion to duty, health, and temperament. If she passes all these tests she may be invited the second time. At the second invitation the man may be more serious about the marriage. In some African countries a man meets a girl through introduction by friends or relatives. A few men meet girls by themselves either in the schools or in the marketplace, before the girl is invited home.

> A Zulu young man makes no dates, but instead, surprises a young woman by waiting for her at a water hole, on the road to the store--using the best phrases and oratory he can muster, he tells her of his home for her. Now that young men do not find time to pursue a girl in this way, their sisters often take over and woo other girls on their behalf. [12]

African customs allow the man to have as many wives as he so desires, provided he observes the prescribed method of obtaining them. Like most other twentieth-century women the African woman regards herself as neither a slave nor a chattel. But no one could marry a woman without paying a token of appreciation for his troubles in rearing and training a wife. Although many African women are living the life of the present age, the majority of them are living in a past age.

In most African tribes marriage involves the payment of a bride price from the groom's family to the bride's family. The sum of money varies from tribe to tribe. In the

Igbo tribe the estimated rate is only around $90. The bride
price is often a financial burden to the groom's family, but
it is a symbol of love and consequently gives both families
an oath of allegiance in keeping the marriage intact.   This
custom has often been misunderstood.   It should not only be
regarded as a cash payment for personal property, and a
token of appreciation, but as a security fund in case a woman
wants to leave her husband.   A woman may recall her dowry
rituals, and may therefore consider staying with her
husband, instead of deserting him.   In a Moslem African
society women are more restricted in their houses in marriage.   The woman is usually placed in exclusive seclusion in
her husband's house.

> The wives of the Hausa ruling class experience
> the most restrictive form of marriage, "Auren
> Kulle. "   This is marriage of complete seclusion
> in which a woman may never go outside the con-
> fines of her husband's compound.   Many of the
> household duties are carried out by servants, and
> social contact and common interests between hus-
> band and wife are minimal. [13]

As previously mentioned, the African woman maintains
certain acres of gardening for emergency around the compound.
The pattern of rural life usually consists of more than one
nuclear family.   All the family members cooperate in the
pursuit of agriculture, in religious ceremonies, in marketing,
and in the education of their children.   "There results a
strong sense of kin obligation and dependence.   One shares
with one's relatives, one grows strong and safer through having many family ties that are actively functioning. "[14] All
food crops grown around the compound are regarded by tradition as a privilege, and the African woman cherishes her
family's privilege regarding the village compound.   Families
who migrate to the urban areas are seen as being deprived
of this special privilege.

In the early twentieth century African women's education was mainly in the domestice sciences of cooking and
needlework.   Various orientation courses gave the girls a
very sound and satisfactory knowledge and kept them well
disciplined in accordance with native custom.   In the middle
of the twentieth century, however, one saw the emergence
of different types of African women.   The influence of church-
oriented schools and domestic centers has increased the educational opportunities for women.   With increased women's

education in Africa the problems of rigid subordination and
complete seclusion are effectively being challenged.

The sex ratio of students varies from country to country.   The numbers of women who went to school increased
after Independence, but the numbers of females who went to
school did not compare with the male enrollments.   In Nigeria the gap is narrowing since the introduction of universal primary school.   In the postprimary schools the ratio
of female students is comparing favorably with that of the
males.   Girls' institutions mainly provide the students with
domestic and moral education, while their male counterparts
are aimed toward academic careers.

In Ivory Coast as in Cameroun, girls are oriented toward becoming seamstresses, beauticians,
and home economists.   In commercial fields, they
are concentrated in typing rather than accounting
and they are more often found in short than in long
cycles of technical studies. [15]

While the Christian churches have in a sense
liberated some Nigerian women by providing, through
their schools, the opportunity for women to become
economically active, this has also occurred in the
context of households in which women are isolated
from a female support system with its own viable
economic base. [16]

The traditional African philosophy of education was
that book knowledge was a power and such a power should
be reserved only for the males, who will inherit the land.
Hence the whole area of women's education was beset with
difficulties.   As far as the Western type of education was
concerned, African culture usually allowed only men to have
the advantage of formal education.

During the precolonial and colonial eras university
education for females was so inaccessible that few parents
could send their daughters.   Even after Independence only a
few privileged females went to a university.   Most of those
who were educated fully by their own parents came from
well-to-do families.   After Independence, when the governments of each country started to offer scholarships and fellow-
ships, women began to have the opportunity to attend a university.   However, due to their population in the postprimary
schools, fewer women attended universities than did males.

"Finally, despite the long history of educational development in the Cameroun, women there are not proportionately more numerous in universities than their Ivory Coast counterparts (the ratio of male to female university students is 13.1 in the first case but only 11.1 in the second one)."[17]

In many African countries statistical limitations have made up-to-date figures impossible to obtain; sometimes census figures obtained are inaccurate and unreliable.

From all corners of Africa, women's voices have been clamoring for economic improvement and educational opportunities. In a little over a decade women have achieved remarkable positions in their societies. Unfortunately, however, the greater proportion of them are still practicing subsistence farming in the rural areas. The introduction of education has lifted many women to the rank of judges, merchants, educators, ministers of state, traditional chiefs, medical doctors, and lawyers. In this way African women play a very important part in raising living standards for the entire population and in achieving economic development that is compatible with the social fabrics and traditions of their community.

There are still certain areas in Africa where impediments to formal education are raised. In Moslem cultures where strict seclusion of women is practiced the Western type of education at times may be impossible. Many Moslem parents encourage their daughters to attend the Koranic institutions first. "They often feared, for example, that Western education would teach children to be disrespectful to their elders. Thus in the ancient Moslem schools of the western Sudan, children sat or knelt before their teachers as a sign of respect. However, the new European schools taught children to stand when speaking to a teacher."[18]

Often when a new change is introduced the change agent is looked upon with suspicion and hostility. This was what happened in the early colonial era. When it was established that education provided an opportunity for advancement to the "new Eve" parents changed their minds and allowed their daughters to go to school. However, despite all efforts made by some African governments to persuade women and children to go to school many areas are uninterested in the programs. "Nigeria is an example of this kind of situation; about 80 percent of children in the southern areas of the country are attending primary school but this figure drops to about 10 percent in the vast northern region which has over one-half of the nation's children."[19]

Often people's ways of life may be in conflict with government educational-development policies, especially where there is universal primary education, (U. P. E.), as in Nigeria. Nigerian Head of State Obasanjo, speaking at the Dallas Government Girls College at Kano in 1978, blamed the level of discipline in Nigerian society on women's apathy about education. "Mothers wielded influence over their children, and without sound education, young girls could not grow into responsible mothers. Gone are the days when the rightful place for a woman is in the kitchen, because it is now universally accepted that when one educates a woman, one educates a nation. "20

It was not easy to allow girls to attend schools with the boys at the initial stage, but later on parents were delighted to see their daughters joining the chorus with their male counterparts in singing the popular African children's song:

> We are all going to our classes,
> With clean hands and faces,
> To pay great attention to what we are told,
> Or else we shall never
> Be happy forever,
> For learning is better than silver and gold.

Chapter 2

KINSHIP AND SOCIAL ORGANIZATION

African traditional law reflects the subordinate status of African women. Women of the world, like African women, have
realized that the world is mainly for men. Most of the existing cultures have given premiums to males. In the Scrip-
tures the position of women is expressed in the gospel of
St. Paul.

> These very difficult sayings from Talmud, the
> source of post-Biblical Jewish law and custom, sum
> up the position of women in the Jewish tradition.
> They are merely two sides of the same coin. As
> long as the woman followed her prescribed course
> as devoted helpmate to her husband and responsible
> household manager and mother, she was accorded
> great respect. Should she seek to stray from what
> was defined as the female role, however, into the
> male's domain of study and prayer so central to
> Jewish civilization, she was demeaned and often
> ridiculed. [1]

13

The traditional African marriage is a means of pro-
tecting and respecting a woman in her society. Despite the
often-recurring expressions from the elders that its aim is
for procreation, marriage also provides the woman's financial
security.

The husband is supposed to look after the entire family
and to support the wife throughout life. Sex outside marriage,
whether polygamous or monogamous, is taboo; the husband
is responsible for sexual satisfaction of the wife or wives,
while the wives are customarily bound to do all the work at
home. The man owns all the children born in his household.
If a woman decides to leave her husband custom has it that
the woman must surrender the children to him. In cases
where a man dies before the woman, and the children are
still not old enough to care of themselves, the children are
left in the custody of the woman and her relatives.

At times the woman might get some help from other
members of the family, but there are certain chores that
she is traditionally obliged to perform in the compound: preparing the food; keeping the house, her kitchen, and her husband's living room; making the bed; serving her husband;
and going to farm, market, and laundry. In such a way an
African woman accepts the natural dominion of a man over
her. A woman is not usually recognized as a partner in
African tradition. A woman in African society is expected
to be pure until she gets marries. This means she has to
remain a virgin until she puts a fire in her husband's inner
room--a ritual of maturity even with the "new Eve." She
has to remain a virgin until after the church marriage. Traditionally marriage is not intended for pleasure. It is a procreation ritual that is a means of reincarnation. "A hero
must surely return to his family after death." There will
be no way for the dead ancestors to come back to life if
there is no marriage. A spinster and a bachelor are never
recognized. The norms certainly seem to condemn those
who remain single. They are discouraged from staying single
in a society where there is no government support for those
who are old and feeble. Marriage at a young age was once
mandatory, but now girls marry at an older age, mainly because modern African women have started to attend schools
like their male counterparts, since the middle of the twentieth
century. However, there are still a few who marry at the
early age of 14-16 years.

Great honor is given to a married woman. Because

of this, respect is accorded to woman's sexuality and procreation.   Everywhere in Africa the attitude toward women's
menstruation was and still is regarded as an essential norm
and part of cultural mores.   A woman's body is regarded
as taboo for certain periods of the month, and she is regarded as being secret by her husband.   Menstruation is a condition of the wife that is known only to her husband.   A woman
who is seeing her month reduces her daily work.   She re-
frains from going to streams and the market.   Even though
she goes to the stream or river to draw water she must not
take a bath or swim in the waters.

> The menstruating woman was to have no physical
> contact whatsoever with a man.   Like the person
> suffering from a gonorrheal discharge, she was
> impure and to be shunned physically by all males,
> including her husband. [2]

During the period of menstruation the traditional man
regards his wife as secret and impure.   Most African societies put her in seclusion from her husband in her own kitchen,
which is adjacent to her husband's living room.   In a polygamous home a woman's contact depends upon when it is her
turn to visit her husband.   The first lady of the house is
responsible for scheduling who shall see the husband of the
house.   In a few African societies a woman may not speak
openly to her husband during the period when she is regarded
as being secret.   In Moslem societies the period of menstruation is treated with more rigidity.   A woman at this time is
regarded as impure and is therefore left in total seclusion.
The Moslem tradition regards the rigidity of seclusion as a
norm, not only as a hygienic measure.   This period requires
all women to restrict themselves and exercise some modera-
tion and modesty in daily activities.

Married woman braid and plait their hair.   The body
is at times left bare, but more often it is covered with Buba
and wrappers, which look similar to skirts and blouses and
begin at the waist.   Married women usually wear double wrappers, while single women or spinsters wear only a single
wrapper.   Traditional norms require married women to leave
their hair tied, while only a single woman is allowed to cut
her hair short.   Nevertheless, married women cut their hair
short immediately after their husbands are dead.   It is regarded as a sign of mourning to see a married woman cutting
her hair.

Preparation of food is one of the major tasks of African women.   Men are never welcome in the kitchen.   The man must be served with food in order to fulfill the role assigned to him by culture.   The custom requires women to prepare the food for the household, but they have to eat in the kitchen while the "god of all creations" is served.   A birth of a girl is accepted as a good gift from God, and as an enrichment of the home after her bride price is paid. The birth of a male child carries with it great rejoicing-- an arrival of one who is to inherit the land.   In African societies women are given special respect as long as they play their prescribed roles.

> Women who know how to make truth sweet, tender and accessible, make it your task to bring the Spirit of this Council into institutions, schools, homes, and daily life.   Women of the entire universe whether Christian or non-believing, you to whom life is entrusting at this grave moment in history it is for you to save the peace of the world. [3]

The African woman is the architect of moral and spiritual development.   Of course the man is regarded as the master of the house; the term accepted by the women of African society.   Day-to-day feeding is assigned to the women.   The traditional woman never asks her hasband for money to feed the family.   In fact she is often the breadwinner of the household through her agricultural activities.   She objects to the ideas of the "new Eve" who asks her husband for a monthly food budget.

> From her childhood a Nigerian woman is introduced to the pots and pans that are to be her companions for the rest of her life.   I know the African tribe where the woman is expected to stand by her man with a towel on her shoulder with which he would clean his hands until he finished his meal.   Woe betide her if there is too much pepper or salt in the soup.   There are others who have to go down on their knees to offer a glass of water to their husbands. [4]

Ritual at birth is the same whether the child is a male or a female.   A name is given to a new baby by the father when the midwife invites him to see his child.   The father is overwhelmed with joy at the first sight of the baby

if it is a boy, but, on the other hand, if it is a girl he gives
her a name meaning that she will bring money to the family
when she marries.   In Igbo language such names as "Ego"
(money), "Nwakaego" (more than money), "Uba" (riches), and
"Aku" (property) may be used.   After the birth of the baby
naming is regarded as an informal ceremony.   Naming ceremonies, accompanied by traditional rituals, take place after
one week, when the midwife visits for circumcision of the
new baby.   After the birth the mother is confined in the room
with the baby for a period of eight days; the confinement varies
from one country to another.   This is a period of rest because the mother has lost a lot of blood during the delivery.
She is exposed to the public immediately after her child is
circumcised by the midwife.   The circumcision ceremony is
attended by mothers and nearby friends.   The new baby is
often in great pain because the operation is performed under
no anesthetic.   Women sing different ritual songs of consecra-
tion for induction into the world of culture.

        Since some of the babies are delivered in the ortho-
dox hospitals the work of the traditional midwife may be reduced.   A child born in the maternity hospital is circumcised
there before leaving.   Most of the circumcisions in the West-
ern-oriented hospitals are performed on males.   When the
mother returns from the hospital, she approaches the local
midwife for the circumcision if the baby is a female.   In
many African countries circumcision is joyously celebrated
with a dance.

        From birth an African woman is regarded as a simple,
humble creature who is to marry away from home.   She is
a symbol of child rearing and the material world.   Her male
counterpart is honored and respected as one to inherit the
father's land.   Because of assigned roles for males and females certain privileges are allotted only to the male.   These
include the opportunity of going to school and outside employment.   The virtues of spiritual inheritance are generally de-
nied to women.   Certain cultures also do not allow women
to hold hierarchical instruments of authority.   Thus this
spiritual endowment makes women appear inferior as they
are deprived of certain cultural privileges.   Nevertheless,
whatever might be their cultural deprivation women are en-
trusted with caring for the family's morals and the children's
daily needs.   The male traditionally protects and guides the
household's spiritual and long-term material needs.

        You women have always had as your lot the pro-

tection of the home, the love of beginning, and
understanding of cradles. Reconcile men with life
and above all, we beseech you watch carefully over
the future of our race. Hold back the hand of man
who, in movement of folly, might attempt to destroy
human civilization (Vatican Council II, 1965).
   The saying that behind every successful man there
is always a woman is very true in this country. It
can be legitimately argued that both men and women
have mutually witnessed the teething problems that
have confronted or continued to plague this country.
It is therefore lawful to conclude that any lasting
solution to our ills must include the active participation of the women in a positive way. As the
mothers of the nation the unity, peace, and happiness of this country is dear to their hearts. [5]

   Since the colonial days many women in Africa have
aspired to and reached positions of prominence. They belonged to different societies of the market women. Ofttimes
they were nicknamed "Mummy Gold." A few of them have
been: Nwanyi-Oji, the leader of the women's riot in Nigeria
in 1929; Funmilayo Ransome-Kuti, the market women's leader
and politician, 1940; Margaret Ekpo, a member of the Eastern Nigerian Legislature, 1970; Mrs. Nzimiro, merchant;
Mrs. Kalu Ibiam, the leader of the Girl Scouts; Mrs. Buchi
Amacheta, novelist; Adaora Ulasi, writer; Mrs. Rose Njoku,
women's leader; Dr. June Holst-Roness, the mayor of Sierra
Leone; Chief Mrs. Akioninade, elected member of the Con-
stituent Assembly; Madam Carmen Pereira, member of the
Guinea-Bissau National Assembly; Madam Altastes, Ghanian
market woman; and the heroines of Mozambique. These women were very powerful during their political days. They
fought hand in hand with their male counterparts against colonialism. They were formidable in their fights and agitations
because they had a common enemy. "The resistance to Portuguese colonial rule in Angola, Mozambique, and Guinea-Bissau has encouraged the greater mobility to women involved
in the movement" (Rich, 1975).

   In 1929 women organized against the colonial rule in
southern Nigeria. The southern Nigerians fought the administrative officers when they introduced a tax system on women, and this policy was vehemently challenged by all women's
organizations. About thirty-two women were shot and killed,
and about thirty of them were wounded. The mishandling of
women's resistance in 1929 revealed the weakness of the co-

lonial administration in Africa. From that day on all women
on the African continent have increased their search for liberation and identity.

The social and economic roles played by African women,
particularly by the market women, need closer investigation.
Such investigation will help to change their long history of
low position and second-class status.

> Not only did women perform all domestic chores,
> as early as medieval times, and especially in mod-
> ern Eastern Europe from which most American
> Jews originated.... Often they relieved their hus-
> bands entirely of economic responsibilities, so that
> they could devote themselves to the ideal masculine
> pursuit of study. Frequently they made a signifi-
> cant economic contribution to the family by selling
> their home-produced wares in the market place. "[6]

The whole problem of African women's education was
beset with difficulties. Upon the arrival of Western-type education cultural traditions allowed only the male to go to school.
The parents of those girls who wanted to follow the males to
school had a decided interest in acquiring the bride price that
their marriage would bring. The disfavor customarily began
at birth, when arrival of a female child brought disappoint-
ment or dishonor to the families in societies that placed a
premium on male children. With the advent of the missionaries education was open only to male children. "The towns-
people did not want to have their girls educated; their philosophy was that book knowledge was power and that power should
be retained in the hands of men. "[7]

The early twentieth century was a period of transfor-
mation in Africa. Schools were opened to women. For the
first time females began to compete with their male counterparts for certain government jobs. Women's education was
still mainly in domestic science--cooking, needlework, housekeeping, and laundry--but the courses were planned to give
them morals and disciplines in accordance with African culture and traditions. The influence of the Christian churches
was felt tremendously in the education of African women.

The Church of the Missionary Societies and the Roman
Catholic Church competed very strongly for the education of
the women in Africa.

As most of the school children were baptized, the
missionaries considered it much safer to keep them
at the mission house, which served as a show piece
of the new way of life, and thus shielded them from
the pagan environment of the rest of the society.
This was the beginning of the boarding school system that was introduced in the country. [8]

The basic curriculum in the school included Bible
stories, prayers, music, arithmetic, geography, and English.
Simple English was taught, as this was then thought to be
the language of commerce and civilization. The missionaries
adopted a practical scheme to attract the children from the
villages. The few schoolchildren provided with clean and
attractive clothes were made to march around the various
sections of Omtrli Town. [9]

One of the major signs of Christian influence in Africa
was the replacement of polygamy with monogamy. In certain
areas the church built convents where girls--especially those
intending to get married in the church--were kept. They
attended marriage encounter courses and were introduced to
the philosophy of one man/one wife. At times force was
used to gather girls together who were preparing for marriage to stay in the convent until they got married in the
church. This approach was carried out more forcefully by
the Roman Catholic Church than by the Protestant sects.

The C. M. S. operated primary schools as well as
a Women's Training Home in the town. The training home was for the training of wives of mission
agents and other converts. But in 1912 Miss Kate
Beswick, who was in charge of the training home,
became alarmed by the vigorous effort that was
being made by the Roman Catholics to attract the
people of Emii to their own church. [10]

With the increase of women's education in different
fields of learning the subordinate position of women is now
being challenged. Custom permitted African men to have
more than one wife, provided the rituals of obtaining them
were met. Such ideas of plural marriage are no longer being
accepted with good grace. Women's acceptance of the African
man as "god of all creations" in his house does not necessarily
mean that women have no rights of their own. Whatever the
men might think of the women's positions they nevertheless
indirectly govern their respective households. "Our grand-

mothers had women's liberation long before it became popular in the West.   In many African ethnic groups you see the male head issuing orders, but the mother is giving him the instructions," writer Adaora Ulasi[11] has said.   The African women have often been able to resolve many struggles through peaceful demonstrations and radical means.   While men cowardly accepted the direct rule imposed on them by the colonial administrators, women many times demonstrated and fought back to resist adverse laws.   They have, in different African countries, demonstrated against government seizure of land, marketing-board law fixtures, and government takeover of schools.

Women, though considered weak, could not tolerate a few abuses from the colonial government, while sometimes men resignedly implemented them.   Men's cowardly acts might be attributed in part to fears of being victimized by the colonial overlords and their African representatives.   Unlike African men, early Europeans who came to Africa accorded a certain respect to women.   Often they avoided having conflicts with women's market associations, which were and still are the strongest women's organizations in Africa. European colonialists often regarded African men as subhuman and forced them accept their orders at gunpoint.   In order to implement the direct rule of African people the powers of the warrant chiefs and the police and court messengers were strengthened.   Men would dash into the bushes for safety whenever the policemen or court messengers visited the villages, while the women would stay behind to protest any government proposals that were contrary to their way of life. They would demonstrate through their organizations while their husbands were in the bush avoiding arrest.

The hostility between the people and the government was constant.   While the colonial government was forcing its way into the hinterlands the population was often suspicious of their movements.   "Douglas himself admitted that most people in Owerri were decidedly hostile to the government and refused to accept the rule. "[12]

During his travels in Owerri, for example, Bishop Tugwell gathered that Douglas's misrule had engendered a strong dislike for any white man associated with the government.   Because of his harsh and condescending attitute toward the Africans, the District Commissioner was dreaded by the local people (including the chiefs), and his frequent outbursts of temper and obtrusiveness irritated even the colonial office. [13] An eyewitness, A. C. Onyeabo, Bishop Tugwell's catechist,

reported that he saw Douglas in 1905 beating and kicking a
man in the open market without justifiable reason.   The DC
even threatened to arrest him because he deplored his inhu-
man action.   For this reason he was deterred from deliver-
ing a letter from the Bishop to the DC.   Naturally the Bishop
was irritated by Douglas's behavior. 14

The hostile attitudes of such colonial administrators
as Douglas were not acceptable to African women.   They
demonstrated against the government in protest of imposition
of any laws.   At times they met with violence while forcing
their wishes through.

Education of women in the initial period of the arrival
of the missionaries in Africa was beset with difficulties, yet
women were the pillars of the missionaries' evangelization
and education.   They wanted their children, particularly the
males, to learn the white man's education.

It is a historical fact that when the first missionaries came to this country with the message of
God, the Nigerian woman was there with her husband to teach the little ones the rudiments of the
faith.   That our country and the church have made
so much progress today is due largely to the close
and wonderful cooperation of the women. 15

The mother of Isaac Mba, for example, specifically
indicated that she persevered as a Christian amidst
local persecution of Christians because she wanted
to see her son enter the Ministry.   She was disappointed because Isaac was dismissed from his position as a school teacher in 1890 by the English re-
formers. 16

Women's morals and their sense of duty reflect their
positions within the societies.   They continue to attend to
their family's needs, thereby confirming the importance of
women in the family.   In Africa there are still many clubs
or hierarchical institutions that are not open to women.   In
those that are lenient enough to allow them entry the code of
ethics requires them to accept a second-class status.

Polygamy has not completely disappeared from the
African scene.   The "new Eve" is now objecting to the traditional culture that is not in the best interest of the African
patrilineal marriages.   The church marriage has helped to

free women from polygamous marriages.   Most of them have
entered the Christian church only to be the proud possessor
of a husband they will not have to share with other women.
Men who are by nature polygamists accept the culture because
of the freedom of enjoyment it brings.   A few Christian men
in Africa have openly condemned polygamy because of the
problems involved and also ideas based on church law.

Divorce is not easy to obtain in traditional African
marriages.   As long as a women has a male child she has
a root in the African scene.   Even though she may be forced
by her husband to leave the house, it is regarded as a tempo-
rary separation. The children normally will bring their mother
home when they have attained the age of maturity, and certainly when they have reached the age to inherit some of the
family's heirlooms.

> It is generally accepted, however, that if there are
> children of the marriage, some of the property
> should go to them.   The grain in the store or in
> the unripe field can be taken by the husband if there
> are no children, but if there are, food must be
> left for them, and a proportion of the household
> possessions go to them. [17]

> A woman can leave her husband without expressly
> demanding divorce and indeed without necessarily
> wishing for it.   She may hope that he will come
> after her and apologize for whatever has offended
> her. [18]

The "new Eve" usually deserts her children and her
husband for the urban setting.   However, she keeps contact
with her children who are left with her deserted husband.
Because of patrilineal marriages children are left with the
husband when the wife deserts.

> When I look back on the history of our fathers and
> mothers, who proposed and married according to
> the customs and faithfulness, I fear to look at our
> women of today, who just marry out of curiosity
> to divorce tomorrow. [19]

The tradition of the African people does not favor
single women.   In the custom of marriage a woman is duty-
bound to get a husband partly for procreation and partly for
her security.   The only evil that prevents a woman from

getting married is bad manners and personal conduct.   It
goes with the old Igbo saying that "good manners is beauty. "
For a woman to raise her morals she must have a husband.
A home filled with children is regarded as the best home,
because "multitude is power, " according to African ways of
life.   A woman may not have a child in her father's compound.   If by accident a woman becomes pregnant she must
associate the child with a male partner, for it is a great
pride for a child to have a father.   The idea of a single
parent is not welcome in many African societies.   An ex-
ception may be given to a widowed home, where the father
dies and leaves the children in the care of the wife or wives.
In such a case the man's immediate relatives assume the
guardianship until the children are able to take care of themselves.   When a woman marries and has a baby she might
call him "Anii, " meaning "I have joined the family. "

>   The marriage contract too was considered a pro-
>   tective device for women.   It provided for the
>   wife's financial security both within the marriage
>   and in case of divorce or being widowed.   It or-
>   dered her husband to support her and held him
>   responsible, too, for her sexual satisfaction. [20]

Twentieth-century African women have abandoned a
few ideas of their culture, but the characteristics of the
market women have not changed.   The organization is now
more oriented to economic development than pre-Independence
political consciousness.   Because of economic power held
by some of these market women the Western world has recognized their importance.   African women's main problems
seem to differ little from those of women from the Western
world; however, their problems are more concerned with
economic freedom and the "good life. "   In these areas they
are far behind their Western counterparts.

>   Women over half the globe have been but chattels.
>   Wives are bargained for, bought and sold, as other
>   merchandise, and as a consequence of the annihila-
>   tion of their natural rights, they have no political
>   existence.   In Hindustan the evidence of women is
>   not received in a court of justice.   The Hindu wife,
>   when her husband dies, must yield implicit obedi-
>   ence to the oldest son.   In Burma, they are not
>   allowed to ascend the steps of the court of justice,
>   but are obliged to give their testimony outside the
>   building.   In Siberia, women are not allowed to

step across the footprints of men or reindeer.
The Moors, for the slightest offense, beat their
wives most cruelly. The Tartars believe that
women were sent into the world for no other purpose then to be useful and to be slaves. [21]

There is no doubt that this essay has brought to light
a few common arguments on the position of women as charged
by women's leaders everywhere. These African women are
a heterogeneous group with similarities in many areas, but
few of them are completely liberated. About 80 percent of
them are still traditionally oriented. "Women in the rural
areas are subjected to the worst disabilities like illiteracy,
poverty, starvation, scarcity of water, lack of medical care,
and many other obstacles at stake. These women, bound by
their traditional and customary laws, concern themselves only
with domestic work, and upbringing their children. "[22]

Chapter 3

THE MARKET WOMEN

All over Africa the activities of the market women have pene-
trated into the rural areas.   In agricultural systems where
production is undertaken primarily for subsistence marketing,
structures are of secondary significance.   Most of what is
produced on the farms is traded for money; these products
are as vital to the well-being of the farm family as the art
of agricultural production itself.   Women haul the commodities produced on their farms to the nearby markets.   Women
petty traders practice some type of gardening around their
houses during their leisure hours.   Wherever farming is the
main occupation for the family the woman customarily maintains trading as a subsidiary occupation.   The peasant women
depend on the cash realized from the sales of the commodities produced on their farms.

Uchendu's discussion on history of trade among the
Igbos of Southern Nigeria is especially revealing.

Trading has a long history among the Igbos.   Trade

before the European contact was of two types: the
rural village market, which was dominated by women in which exchange was limited to domestic
needs; and long distance trade within or outside
Igbo areas which was dominated by men. [1]

Women's trading activities are less complex than those
of men.   Their way of trading does not rigidly emphasize the
economic principles of supply and demand.   There are different types or grades of trade dominating the scene on each
level.   The difference in the levels may be due to the type
of commodities transacted.   Most of the peasant women traders operate in the nearby village market, where they sell
their fresh produce.   Every town has its own marketplace,
where the sellers and buyers meet every eighth day; the market may meet every day if it operates in rural areas.   The
marketplace is not only a place for economic transactions,
but a place for the women to gossip, a place for burial ceremonies, and a place where both male and female elders meet
for discussions and important rituals.

The marketplace is often an attractive spot, with different types of huts.   A large area is frequently shaded by
trees and surrounded with little open sheds having very low
thatched roofs mounted on rude posts.   Here thousands of
women sit and chat from early morning until late evening.

Women dominate the retail trade.   They are liter-
ally everywhere as buyers and sellers.   Before
marriage, girls are expected to acquire successful
marketing techniques.   Women are good bargain
hunters.   They haggle over prices in a manner
which might frighten Westerners.   They sell their
husband's as well as their own farm products--
yams, palm oil, palm kernels, cassava, okora,
melons and collected products as okazi, otasi
(vegetables). [2]

A century ago in Africa, when goods were bartered,
the cowry shell was used in the market trade in most parts
of West Africa.   The Portuguese brought in the cowry shells
to the marketing ports.   In the early sixteenth century the
king of Portugal issued a license to import cowry shells from
Indies to the West African country of Sao-Tome.   In 1522 the
cowries were imported into Nigeria from the coast of Cala-
bar in the Cross River state.   In the seventeenth century the
bulk of cowries entered into different African countries from

the East Indies.   During this period the flow of cowries increased in West Africa, particularly in Nigeria, but fluctuated
and depreciated in value.   In the nineteenth century the value
of 2, 000 cowries was equal to a few shillings sterling or approximately fifty cents in American money.   The value of
cowries declined even further when quantities were shipped
from Zanzibar into the southeastern area.   In Nigeria in the
1940s, when cowries were replaced by the British coins, the
value of 2, 000-3, 000 cowries was equated with sixpence--
twelve pence sterling or 80, 000 to the pound sterling--or
three dollars in American money.   Cowries were moved in
bags.   They were tied with strings into bunches of fifty, into bunches of 350 (five strings), in beads of 300 (ten bunches),
and bags of 20, 000 (ten heads) weighing over sixty pounds.

Cowries were used easily by the market women in
their exchange of goods, and they found them more handy to
use than when they traded by barter.

Trading by barter lingered on for years in the
same parts of the country, in spite of the Government's efforts to stop it.   Lord says that there is
abundant evidence to show that the attraction of the
apparently double profit to be gained by ignoring
currency as a medium of trade, and selling and
buying in a single transaction, had done much to
destroy trade.   Cowries, manillas, brass, rods,
and copper wires were used until comparatively
recently. [3]

The traditional Barter Economy is associated with
an earlier stage of African history.   It grows naturally out of the African past, and expresses what
Adam Smith called man's natural propensity to
truck, barter, traffic and exchange.   In the more
remote areas and among semi-nomadic groups,
there are few specific market-place sites and inter-
personal transactions form the basis of the market
principle. [4]

The money-barter economy represents a midpoint
along the continuum between the old barter system and the
modern economy.   In this case a rudimentary marketplace
exists and market principles operate.   Peripherally, peasant
women are not dependent on the market for the acquisition of
the basic necessities of life.

Those traders who combine farming and petty trading
are regarded as part-time traders, most of whom are women.
When farm business is not at its peak period men and women
practice some kind of trading.   Unlike the situation in advanced
countries, complementarity of enterprises does not really
exist, so that each peasant farmer trades during the off-season.   This keeps them busy until the return of the busy season.

There are full-time petty traders; most of these men
and women are found in the urban sector of the economy.
They buy most of the commodities from the rural people before they resell them in the daily market.

> While casual or part-time traders operate from
> their homes and are to be found in every settle-
> ment, professional traders are evenly distributed.
> We have already noticed the existence of specialist
> communities in traditional society.   Today the old
> pattern is reflected in two ways.   First, the new
> towns and commercial centres drew their initial
> trading population largely from the traditional trad-
> ing communities. [5]

The third type of trader is the produce-buying agent,
who travels from village markets to central markets on bicycle.   From the local market women he buys palm oil and
palm kernels, which are later resold to produce agents at
the central markets.   He buys produce for his master during
the period of his apprenticeship, and may start on his own
whenever he is able to save enough money.   African petty
traders are known for their individualistic attitude and their
lack of cooperative enterprise.   A petty trader could use an
outside man or cooperate with one, unless that one is his
servant or his agent under an existing system; however, cooperative efforts are mainly nonexistent.

Another type of trader is the importer of foreign commodities.   The exporters and importers of large firms will
be excluded from this analysis because they form a group of
expatriate firms whose activities in African trade are full of
profiteering.   Their main interest is not for the petty traders
and farmers, but for the profit of the foreign traders and
companies.

> Talked yesterday to the head of one of the big
> cocoa combines about the West African growers.

Complaint that the Government had fixed the price
at 15/- ($2.00) per load of 60 lbs. is inadequate
... found him entirely unsympathetic.... The
combined chief arguments were unconvincing. Existing or high prices he claimed would make the
native lazy or encourage in the black market the
goods now in short supply. [6]

The exporters and importers of foreign goods are
mainly men. They operate in such commercial centers as
Lagos, Accra, Freetown, Monrovia, Abidjan, Bouake, and
the central Ivory Coast market. These exporters usually
retain the market women as their main agents, because they
wield much power among their organizations. Interestingly
enough, market women like Proud Mammy, Altastes of Accra, Ghana, was one of those women who was assigned benevolent as well as malevolent powers. These women could
kill or cure with their marketing organizations. As noted
with Hodder and Ukwu, these organizations vested many men
and women with political power and frequently their women
members with basic agricultural and marketing means. Yao
Aduamah of West Africa observed in 1978:

The Accra market mammies were proud of Madam
Altastes, Secretary and talked as though they were
the co-owners of his new tape recorder. ... we
come on now said the market secretary, we better
prepare and send our resolutions to the makers of
photographer's lens covers and the grocer's bucket
handle and my tape machine through the International Conference on Quality Control and enforce-
ment of standards which is to be held in our own
country on May 16.... [7]
With the great clarion call of self-reliance ring-
ing everywhere in the West African countries we
must think about homes and our local manufacturers.
By adherence to standards our manufacturers can
help to refashion consumption styles currently swung
toward foreign goods and commodities and thus save
some foreign exchange. [8]

Many African countries now fully realize the importance
of positions taken by the market women in the improvement
of standards and the goods exported or manufactured for home
cottage industries. From their different villages the market
women receive information on the movable items and their
information is fed back to the manufacturers or their representatives.

A number of sources document the contention that African women have been the reason for the market at Bonake, central Ivory Coast, always being well stocked.   The Abidjan correspondent emphasized the outstanding attraction of foreign investments.   His findings were reported in West Africa:

> Ivorian wealth (Ivory Coast) has been accumulated through the successful development of cocoa, coffee, pineapple and ground nut production, to name but some of the most important ingredients of Ivory Coast's diversified agricultural economy.   They are, however, aimed at foreign markets. . . .   Similarly, coffee is sold in the form of roasted coffee beans in the country and yet Nescafe imported from Europe fills the shelves in the supermarkets in any form.   The development of the Arabusta--a hybrid of the arabica and robusta coffee strains--is an enterprising experiment. [9]

The licensed importers and exporters also buy from the local firms and then resell to their customers in the neighborhood, through the women agents.   Some market women in Africa advertise their goods in their individual market stalls, which they operate in different cities.   A few small importers own stores where they retail some of their imported goods in almost the same way as in the marketplace.   However, the market women also establish marketplaces with their local agents in the rural areas, where certain European manufactured goods are exchanged for African arts and crafts. The marketplaces are vital for the meeting of the buyer and seller, for here they meet face to face.   In the market regular and adequate customer relationships are maintained.

> Women who live in sparsely settled areas of the city and cannot establish a stall in the market must develop compensatory mechanisms if they are to insure regular and frequent interaction with a large number of customers. [10]

A foreign company's agents, who make daily visits to the marketplace, are there to gain new customers.   They bring a few samples of their textiles for dressmakers.   Dressmaking, sewing, and weaving courses are very popular in many of the central markets.   Dressmaking is regarded as valuable to those girls who are unable to attend schools or to those who have passed the age of attending the elementary school.   A few huts or stalls are turned into sewing institu-

tions. Such places help young girls learn how to operate a
sewing machine, something that most African girls love to
do. Some families encourage their daughters to sew, in
order to fulfill their real purpose in life--becoming wives
and mothers. Sewing is a sign of preparation to be a good
homemaker. After the sewing training these women may
marry and have their own children. Some of them will continue in the sewing profession in order to make an economic
and cultural contribution to their society. After completing
her training, each seamstress may then decide to open her
own sewing institution in order to train other girls. The
importation of certain essential consumer goods, such as
cloth, sewing machines, and spare parts for them, will thus
be increased.

Some twentieth-century African mothers do encourage
their children to go to school and get a proper education
rather than crowding into the sewing institutions. In 1960
there were a great many African girls in elementary and
teachers' training institutions and craft centers. Yet there
were many mothers who felt strongly that too much education
would turn their daughters away from their family duties.
These mothers are still ignorant of the fundamental elements
of women's liberation.

> Frequently, it was their mothers who became the
> mediating force between old world cultural attitudes
> of the male population toward educating women and
> the new educational opportunities opening up for
> women which they wanted their daughters to take
> advantage of. [10]

This generation saw African girls in the universities
pursuing various professions; they are no longer solely in the
domestic-science institutions. Does professional ethics remove those university women from participation in their civic
groups? The answer is no! In Africa an education does not
alienate a woman from her civic responsibility. Besides the
religious grouping, of Moslem, Christian, or other sect, the
strongest women's organization is the market women's group.
It draws membership from all tribes and ethnic groups and
is the strength that gives women their political power.

When one enters into an African marketplace one thing
that strikes a visitor's eye is the number of women buying
and selling. Not only do they outnumber males, but they
compete with them in all areas of retail goods, particularly

in consumer-good items. At Ibadan, Onitsha, Accra, Benin,
Monrovia, Boaka, and Abidjan they sit in groups from morning until evening, selling perishable foodstuffs, such as vegetables, palm oil, yams, cassava, garri, pineapples, tobacco,
rice, and fish (both fresh and dried). Most of them operate
in the feeder market. Those who live in the rural areas buy
from the local periodic markets and then retail the commodities in the local daily markets. While the market is in session, there are a number of women, particularly the teenagers,
who go around as hawkers, selling cooked dishes and drinks.
This is one way of advertising the particular goods in the
market.

> Palm oil, salt and rice are bought mostly by Dioula
> women, and carried to minor markets where they
> are retailed. But an increasing number of Guro
> women are engaging in this profitable business, es-
> sentially women living in villages closer to the ma-
> jor markets. Women selling such commercialized
> products cluster together in the market. All palm
> oil merchants sitting in a row, etc. This makes
> it possible to distinguish at a glance the imported
> food stuffs from the native ones. [12]

African women have their own personal rights, such
as the right to own a farm, a piece of land, or to farm their
husband's plot of land, as well as the absolute right to sell
and buy in the marketplace, all of which activities are performed with the permission of their husbands.

After the day's work in the market, the women return
home to prepare pounded foo-foo of garri (cassava starch)
or yams, with soup made from dried fish, melon seeds, or
leaves. In the families where polygamy exists the women
will first serve the food and then visit their husbands, always
serving their husbands. After the day's toil the "lords of all
creation" often sit in their solitary state outside their huts,
waiting to be served by their wives. However, modern educated African women are going through cultural changes. The
influence of education as well as contacts with foreign women
have helped change the status of women tremendously.

Two types of marriage are now common in African societies. Both the church and the courthouse weddings are
contracted only after the completion of the traditional ceremonies. The Moslem marriages are contracted according to
Koranic theology.

She marries in her own right and manages her
trading capital and her profits as she sees fit.
Though women are not the normal instruments
through which land rights are passed, and though
their vertical residence after marriage makes it
impossible for them to play some important social
and ritual roles in their natal village, yet they can
have households, take titles and practice medicine. 13

African women's powers appear now to have been finally recognized.   Their movements have been increased
through their regional organizations.   From Nigeria to Guinea-
Bissau to Mozambique women hold conferences through their
different associations, clubs, and cooperatives.   Davidson
writes:

In the specific context of Mozambican society and
of Portuguese colonialism (notably backward in many
ways, but essentially no different from any other
form of colonialism), the conference attacked the
disabilities of women.   They found, for instance,
that illiteracy has a particularly high incidence
among women who were doubly exploited in traditional and in colonial society, which instilled in
women a feeling of inferiority and dependence and
which conditioned women merely to please men and
run a household. 14

Trades of various consumer goods, ranging from
hawking to operating retail stores, have opened women's eyes
to the answer to the question posed by Anne Kinney in 1903
--"What does a woman want?"   No longer do they just clean,
bake, wash, sew, and nurse, but they are facing the challenges
of the twentieth-century liberation movement.   They are the
sole agents of cosmetic firms, haberdashery firms, textile
firms, and major provision stores.

The correspondence and other agents at Lagos
keep their Igbo land and contacts informed of latest
arrivals in Lagos and often buy and store goods for
them to come and collect.   With the correspondents
and agents in the northern and western regions the
relationship is symbiotic.   The traders based in
Igbo land send off yams, palm oil, garri, and second hand clothing and get in return kola nuts and
Yoruba cloth from the west or grains, fish, meat
and onions from the north. ...   In the retail trade

in imported goods, the few pioneers are dealers
in fashionable clothing and jewelry.... [15]
    The small Nigerian shops in Agbeni street on
the other hand, sell a much wider variety of goods,
though again imported non-perishable goods dominate. Agbeni street is in fact the chief street for
African shopkeepers in Ibadan.... More recently
small Nigerian shops have spread farther westwards
and northwards along Amunigun and Onirekee streets. [16]

The market place is the site where buyers and
sellers meet. African market places are commonly
located at crossroads, lorry parks, railway stations
and centres of transport and labor concentration.
The economic activities of the market place are
regulated by a market principle; it involves the
operation of price mechanism by the forces of
supply and demand. This market principle regu-
lates the production and distribution of goods for
local consumption as well as the export and import
of commodities which form a part of the world net-
work of trade. [17]

    Women's interests in the cosmetic circles have re-
sulted in a tremendous change in the marketplace. It is a
progressive era for African women, who see the unrest created by the romantic-undercurrent lovers who roam the marketplaces in search of girlfriends. African women receive
innumerable suitable social cues to guide them into their
proper roles as women, and to reinforce appropriate behavior. They must dress well and wear their best golden orna-
ments and bracelets in order to show their charms and beauty
to the best advantage. At times diamonds shine from their
ears; diamond rings sparkle on every finger. Many of them
look like vulgar, pretentious prostitutes, but a closer look
will surely reveal that most are typical African women who
look like animated cloths, for they often put on a pair of
slippers.

    Thorstein Veblen equates the terminology and duties
of women. He said,

Vicarious leisure and consumption. They must
continue to run their households, but they must
do so in a manner that reflects the wealth of
their husbands. The more leisure (obtained by
being freed from domestic tasks by servants) they

have, the more they enhance their husbands.   Their
roles as ladies must complement their husbands'
financial position; by conducting themselves pro-
perly, they become assets.

Three Typical African Markets--A Profile

I. Yoruba Traditional Market

The town of Ibadan is considered to be the largest in Africa,
south of the Sahara, with a population of approximately one
million people.   It contains both the traditional native stores
and European shopping centers.   In it is found an example
of a daily market in an important urban center.   Ibadan is
linked with Lagos (the capital of Nigeria), the eastern region,
the ancient city of Benin, and the northern region.   It is
crossed by an important railroad connecting it with Lagos,
Enugu, Port Harcourt, and Kaduna.   Ibadan is associated
with both periodic and central markets.   The periodic markets are attended by producers and consumers from distant
areas.   The number of periodic markets seen in one area
or ring is due to the density of markets in Ibadan.   Some
rings contain five to ten periodic markets because of the
population involved.   Often periodic markets in the Ibadan
area specialize in a particular food, such as crops or vegetables, which are made available to Ibahan from time to
time.

In the Ibadan community most of the markets are daily,
and operate in three intervals--morning session, day session,
and evening session.   The morning market starts very early--
around 5 a. m.   Various vegetables, fruits, wrapping leaves,
oil, cassava, yams, and plantains are sold.   Casual women
traders, who buy in the morning market and then resell in
the day market, dominate the scene.   The morning markets
are used to feed the day and evening markets.

> The dominance of certain other commodities in
> these morning feeder markets reflects the districts
> from which the farm women come.   Elekuru market
> for instance is noted for palm oil and lies at the
> junction ... leading from the main palm oil pro-
> ducing areas to the southwest of the town.   These
> morning feeder markets, however, are rarely sup-
> plied from more than eight miles away and are al-
> most invariably attended only by women head-loading
> their goods into market. [18]

The day market is open from about 10 a. m. until
6:30 p. m. , and operates every day, including Sunday.   It
contains about 6, 000 sellers and is visited by about 50, 000
people in a day.   This type of market is usually located
near railway stations, lorry parks, and commercial centers.
There are certain social customs prevailing in the day market.   Because of the location advantage, the prices are often
inflated.   If one is a foreigner, especially a European, the
prices are doubled.   At the end of each month, particularly
on payday, the prices of the commodities are higher than
normal, because the workers, in both government and commercial establishments, pay off their debts on this day.   With
cash in hand, they buy new goods for themselves and their
families.   The day market then becomes the main source of
income for many groups in the socioeconomic structure:
sellers and producers, market managers, and subsidiary occupational groups.

The third type of market is the Ibadan night market,
which is open from 6:30 p. m. until around midnight and can
hold up to 1, 500 people at one session; however, there are
few such markets in operation around the community.   The
aim of this type of market is to sell prepared foods and petty
articles to the public, and leftover vegetables to the neighborhood.   Most of the time the prices of the food sold at night
are cheaper than those sold during the morning or day markets.   The morning feeder markets supply fresh foodstuffs,
which are prepared and then resold in the night markets.

> Many of these women then spend the rest of the
> day processing the food stuffs into ready made
> dishes (Bean Bread, Eko, Amala, Ebo or (Dodo)
> for sale in their local night market; or they may
> simply break down their purchases into small units
> for resale at perhaps 1d, 3d, or 6d a unit.   This
> kind of night market, in which women connect their
> local communities with the town's main sources of
> food stuffs, can only be understood in the context
> of local Yoruba habits of public feeding.   The bulk
> of the working class eats food that has not been
> prepared in their own homes. [19]

II.   Igbo Traditional Market

An Igbo village is composed of many compounds, each having
a localized patrilineage living in each home.   Each village

may have up to 1,000 men, women, and children.   A village
has its own marketplace, where the community meets once
a week, for Christmas, and for burial ceremonies.

> The circulation of goods and services is only one
> function of the market place; it is also the focal
> point of many social activities and ways of life.
> It is a common activity and way of life.   It is a
> common ground, a meeting place for people and
> authorities and a forum of public opinion....
> When market places are under the jurisdiction of
> traditional authorities, they also serve as judicial
> and religious centers. [20]

Each group that makes up a village has certain things
of common interest.   The population that lives in the village
can trace its blood relationship from one kindred.   The social life is organized within the framework of the village
group.   Rituals and reciprocal gift exchanges, redistributive
sharing, periodic meetings, and common festivals keep the
solidarity of the group alive.   The economy is organized
within the same context.   The farming calendar is set for
the group, and usually runs from the date of bush burning
until the date of the yam harvest festival.

Almost all markets are located in the rural areas.
The Igbo market is held every four or eight days, with each
market day being regarded as a special day usually set aside
for the goddess of the town.   This day is one of feasting and
merriment, when people do no farm work.   Shrines posted
in the marketplace guard against theft or poisoning of food
supplied in the market.   In case such an evil happening oc-
curs, it is believed that the gods or the goddesses of the
market will inflict a supernatural punishment on the person
harming the food.

The concept of periodicity is associated with the structure of the Igbo calendar.   One Igbo year is made up of thirteen lunar months (between twelve and thirteen moons), because the use of moons is easier than a calendar for the
large population of illiterates.   They count from one harvest
month to the next harvest month.   The four-day week and the
eight-day week are traditionally popular, four being a lucky
number.   A native medicine man who predicts the future during his ritual drama counts one, two, three, and four.   At
the end of four figures he either continues up to eight figures
or returns from the fourth figure to the first figure.   The

kola nut, a symbol of hospitality, is usually broken into two
or four layers before it is presented to the group or to a
guest. The figure four repeats in the liturgy of the native
priests and in the reincarnation of witchcraft. Igbo rituals
are more ecological than chronological. A day is Obuchi;
a week is Izu; a month is Onwa; and Aro is one year. Eight
days make one Izu, which is associated with one market day.
In the rural community there are four-day markets and eight-
day markets. The count starts with Eke, Orie, Afo, and
Nkwo, which is a four-day Izu period. After an eight-day
Izu period, the counting is then repeated.

The daily markets are located mainly in the urban
areas or centers like Onitsha, Aba, Enugu, Owerri, and
Nsukka. This type of market is situated in the heart of the
business community. Before the University of Nigeria was
sited at Nsukka the town had a four-day market. When the
university opened in 1960 Nsukka became a university city,
and with the high purchasing power of the people at the university the urban market became a daily market.

Nsukka is a division of the East Central State of Nigeria, at the border of the former eastern region with the
northern region. It is situated on a hill and has cool air
all year. The population in 1963 was 689,353, with an area
of 1,314 square miles; the population density is 342.

Long-distance foodstuffs travel from the Enugu area,
forty miles away, and from Ida, fifty miles from the northern
region. The market at Nsukka is sited on the main road
leading to the capital city of the eastern region. The market is customarily open from early morning until late evening,
and holds an average of 7,000 people daily. There are other
traditional markets located two miles from the daily Nsukka
market, namely Orie-Oba and Nkwo-Ibagwa. These are four-
day markets, where commodities may be obtained at a cheaper price. There are also many eight-day markets in the
Nsukka area.

Retail trade in both daily and periodic markets in Igbo
land is dominated mainly be women. The most popular foods
found in these markets are bottles of palm oil, dried fish,
garri, yams, cassava, ground nuts, cube sugar, sticks of
cigarettes, kola nuts, live chickens, bean cake (Manyi-Manyi),
and bean doughnuts (Akara Ball).

Some areas of the market are reserved for men, who

sell goats, cows, bags of rice, sheep, and palm wine (fer-
mented wine tapped from the palm groves). In these markets
standardized units of measurement are hard to find. Sometimes normal cigarette cups for measuring rice and garri
are reduced in size. Often milk cups are used instead of
cigarette cups, which means that twenty cups of rice or garri
in the market may be only twelve cups at home.

> Weights and measures are more or less absent,
> although in many parts of the continent standard
> weights and measures have appeared in the last
> few decades. The quart beer bottle, the stan-
> dardized cigarette tin, the standardized four gallon
> kerosene tin, and an empty 30-30 shell casing are
> all used measures. There are others. There are
> also many non-standardized units of measurement. [21]

Most of the traders are casual people who crowd the
market during the off-season on the farm: women with little
tables under the trees and men in the market stalls, buying
and selling at a profit along the complex continuum of trading
relationships to the peasants in the rural villages. There
are different types of traders, ranging from distributors of
European manufactured goods to itinerant hawkers. A discussion of market institutions and marketplaces is not complete in Igbo land without a mention of the Onitsha wholesale
market.

III.   Onitsha Market

Like the Ibadan market in the west, Onitsha market is the
largest of all the markets in the eastern region. Onitsha
market is located on the bank of the River Niger. Some
1,150 square miles in area, Onitsha has a population of
797,386 (1963 census). It is interregional in character because it is attended by people from the northern, western,
and midwestern regions. It is attended daily by not less than
100,000 people. "The £500,000 Onitsha market now under
construction is located at a strategic position on the River
Niger."[22]

Good telecommunications and transport systems link
Onitsha with other regions. Such commodities as ground
nuts, tanning goods, dyeing stuffs, pottery, tobacco, cotton
goods, and beans arrive from the northern region via Enugu
by railroad and by lorry via Nsukka. Vegetable oil, cocoa

products, butter, fiber bags, cigarettes, canned fruits, and
wrapping leaves come by road across the River Niger to the
market; vegetables, fruits, woven cloth (Akwete), cement,
and palm products arrive from different areas in the eastern
region.

Many different types of imported goods brought by the
agents of foreign firms are seen in the Onitsha daily market.
These include assembling plants, terrazzo tiles, zinc, textiles (both imported and locally manufactured), glassware,
carvings, saw milling, rubber and crepe supplies, kerosene,
palm oil, press parts, and haberdasheries of all types.   The
important position of Onitsha on the bank of the great river
gives it a location advantage.   There are many middlemen
operating in the market channel, who represent the interests
of the European producers, often to the disadvantage of the
peasant consumers.   The Onitsha marketing system could be
traced from a simple wholesale market to a petty retail shop,
presented in a single diagram showing stages from elementary
to complex marketing insitutions.   The importation of agricultural consumer goods from the rural areas to Onitsha market constitutes an important source of food supply.

The Women's Riot of 1929

A discussion of the activities of the market women in Nigeria
would be incomplete without the mention of the Women's Riot
of 1929.   Igbo women were the movers and shakers behind
the uprising that culminated in the largest women's riot in
Africa's history.   It showed to the world that big things could
be done in the way of organization, that large masses of women could be marshaled, and great forces of resistance called
forth.   It was, in essence, the transfer and application of
European laws to the people whose beliefs and ways of life
were different.   The colonial administrators were mostly responsible to the metropolitan powers and not to the natives,
and the laws were handed to the people by the colonial masters to represent various interests.   Africans who protested
the direct-rule system were called agitators, demonstrators,
blackies, picketers, malcontents, and warriors.   Movements
in various countries were restricted or banned, and sometimes
agitators were deported or exiled.   Arbitrary taxation was
often imposed in many forms, without letting the people know
the use to which the money was put.   It was the management
(and mismanagement) of the colonial administrators that brought
all sorts of harassment, abuse, and beatings to Igbo women.

Women in Africa, particularly those from southeast Nigeria, are physically very strong, due to the hardships they have had to endure. Women may walk about ten miles in search of a profitable trade. They lift and carry on their heads a basket of cassava and yams or a bag of garri to the marketplace for sale. This is the only way they can make money for the household and provide for their children. Considerable control over women is exercised by women's associations and the courts. As they are responsible for the day-to-day feeding of their families, the women may exert a strong influence over men and bring the sanctions of female ancestral spirits to bear upon them. Women will also resort to strikes, ridicule, and cursing if they have no formal means of gaining their ends. The widespread riots of 1929 will long stand as an example of the unity, power, and determination that Igbo women can display.

The Women's Riot of 1929 was a challenge to colonial administrators and made them reverse their method of direct rule. Since they underrated the power of women in Nigeria, they expected any uprising to come from men, as African women are traditionally under their husbands' control. Status was accorded to the male, seniority by birth, irrespective of sex, polygamous family, or agnatic emphasis. Because of this, men were expected to lead or reject any new changes. The native laws were enforced by male rulers, chiefs and priestly elders, with regard to levies and taxes. Land rights, for instance, were thought of as originating from the sanctified ancestors and gods, whom it would be sacrilegious to disobey.

In 1928, when the law mandating that adult men pay a flat tax was enforced for the first time in the eastern provinces by the former British administrative officers, the male population was not happy about it, could not oppose it. The result was that many men deserted their homes and established new homes in the bush, waiting for the census count to be over.

> A proportion of the tax was assigned to the native administration, the balance being paid to the Protectorate Government but the collection was invariably left to the native administration. The most serious obstacle experienced in Nigeria, when the tax was inaugurated, was the difficulty of suppressing personation. A credulous and illiterate people, long accustomed to oppression, were easily victim-

ized by any scoundrel who, producing an old envel-
ope picked up in a deserted camp or even a piece
of newspaper as his credentials, would declare
himself to be the authorized emissary of the government and demand what he chose. [23]

In every province the news of tax proposals was not
received warmly. Men were forced to pay and many of them
who were unable to pay the tax were arrested by the District
Court messengers and detained until they were able to pay.
Sometimes they were handcuffed and their hair shaved off.
At times their wives pawned everything in the house in order
to raise money to pay the tax before the men were released.
This type of rule continued for a time, until it was planned
that women would be taxed also. The argument was that
women were the main source of physical income because of
their activities in the marketplace. They made more money
than men, fed the households, and maintained them. It was
proved that the average Igbo woman before the Riot wore
around her waist, under her wrapper (waist cloth), enough
money to pay the tax levy for five adults. This information
seemed to justify the proposal that "what is good for the
goose is good for the gander. "

The women from Oloko in Aba Division suspected that
they would be taxed like the men, so they organized immediately to resist the proposal. Women all over were dissatis-
fied with the proposal of assessment of their personal property. The Igbo mentality was very complex on the question of
women, so that a solution well adapted to European needs
was not adequate for Nigeria. How could one correctly assess the property of women and the position they held in
southern Nigeria? They were honored members of society,
and accepted their lot with philosophic calm, even with cheer-
fulness, while at the same time were subordinate to the men,
their "lords and masters. " While the men tolerated the in-
justices of taxation with very bad grace, the women smiled
at each other and said the hell with the tax. In assessing
the property of the women, it was necessary to assess the
property of their male counterparts twice. Everything a
woman had belonged to her husband; according to Igbo custom,
a woman had no property. So the women proceeded to organize their resistance from division to division.

The riot spread throughout Igbo land in 1929. All the
women of taxable age joined the protest. They were armed
with machetes, sticks, hoes, palm leaves, and bamboo rods,

singing and chanting the war songs.   Through grass and bush
paths and dripping palms, they came chanting noisily.   They
waved their machetes in their hands and wound palm leaf
"omu" around their elbows.   This alone caused the British
administrators to stare, for an African woman is seldom
seen with a machete.   All roads were closed to traffic with
barricades of trees and palm leaves.   This was only one
way of confronting the Europeans, since they were at this
time the only group that used the roads or drove cars.

Not only did these women attack the Europeans, but
they battled with khaki-clothed court messengers and with
the native policemen standing at attention in gorgeous uniforms
guarding the government houses.   The chiefs, elders, and
tax collectors watched all these moves made by the women.
The chiefs liked the white masters and were in hiding in order to avoid mal-treatment by the mob.   The women organized themselves into groups of hundreds in order to overcome
any attacks by the local court administrators.

They sang war songs like "Enyi Mba Enyi" (People of
Elephant Strength); "Nzogbu, Nzogbu" (Smash, Smash, Smash);
and "Anyi Ga Emeri" (We Will Overcome).   Whenever a group
of these women arrived at the marketplace they would be en-
tertained by the local young women of nontaxable age.   Fail-
ure to receive these women upon their arrival would be followed by a violent attack on the village or town.   For a
town to avoid this sanction an arrangement was made ahead
of time, so that the rioting women were awaited a mile a-
way from any nearby village.

When the women came near the European areas, they
sang songs explaining the cost of running their farm.   Commodities when added up could not meet the cost of the local
tax.   This was the popular song: "The basket of cassava
which is our power and strength is now five cowries. "   Like
the Europeans, the chiefs and elders saw all this confusion
as a sign of mismanagement and they requested strong power
to quell the internal disorder.

> The Lugardian principle of local administration,
> the so-called Indirect Rule, had so seriously dis-
> rupted and disorganised indigenous administration
> that people sought every available means to cir-
> cumvent the unscrupulous exploitation by the govern-
> ment through the warrant chiefs. [24]

The British administrators acted as change agents in a culture they did not understand. They introduced a tax system as though they were administering a local government in their native country. They could not understand that Igbo people in general resent the word "debt" or the payment of a levy. The philosophy behind the owing of a debt has some impact on the life of people in the rural areas. If one cannot pay, one is advised to refrain from buying. Despite the use of the money lenders in the rural areas, the debt collectors were traditionally dreaded. They were called "cock crow" (osu-ube okeokpa), meaning that they arrive and tap at the door before the cock crows early in the morning. According to Igbo custom, debt is not a good thing to mention early in the morning. It brings bad luck to the debtors, especially when the debt collector comes with palm leaves. The women were not able to pay the amount of money proposed by the colonial administrators. On the other hand, they could not owe a debt, as has already been indicated, because that would be contradictory to native custom.

> In 1929, owing to dissatisfaction with the existing native administrations and the unfounded fear that women were going to be taxed, there were serious disturbances, generally known as the women's risings or the "Aba riots" in the Owerri and Calabar provinces. Troops had to be employed in support of the police and many women were killed or injured before order was restored. These disturbances resulted in a reorganisation of the native administration in the areas affected to base them more closely to the indigenous customs of the people. [25]

The mishandling of women resisting in 1929 revealed the weakness of the British administrative machinery in the colonies at that time. With a strong force recruited, thirty-two women died and about thirty-one were wounded. After a thorough investigation by the home government in England into the cause of the riot the native administration was overhauled so as to allow the natives more voice in the local government. The colonial administrators then decided to reverse the roles for a change. There were many reforms in the native courts, which opened the door to indirect rule. The native courts, now the customary courts, were allowed to examine laws and determine their validity according to native laws and customs.

Nevertheless, palm products are Nigeria's leading
cash crop, and had been the country's primary export item, following slavery.   A modus vivendi was
eventually worked out, after the Aba riot of 1929
with the multitudinous clan and village heads, the
natural rulers, who then replaced the warrant chiefs,
the latter having been directly appointed by the British.   Thus the people of the Eastern Region, with
those of the north and west by the end of the nineteenth century shaped to a colonial social economy. 26

Chapter 4

CONTEMPORARY AFRICAN WOMEN

On the vast continent of Africa women are not a homogene-
ous group. There are different people with varied cultures,
but in many areas the cultures are similar. In the early
period of the slave trade most of these African women were
not exposed to outside influences, except those in the coastal
areas, and in fact this contact was something only recently
realized.

Little is known about Africa's early period and its
various cultures. Because of the advantages given to males
by most of the world's cultures women were often suppressed
and their culture distorted. "Where materials on women are
available one still has to contend with the cultural distortions
so evident in the writings of Western social scientists and
visitors to Africa."[1] West African women are strong individuals against whom alien European values were used to measure and interpret their African culture.

The previous chapters have explained in detail the

system of marriage, which is similar in many African countries. The marriages are mainly patrilineal, while the societies are patriarchal and patrilocal. The marriage arrangements are made so that men become the accepted heads of the societies. The marriage becomes legal only after the payment of the bride price, which is a token of appreciation for the loss of the daughter. "Marriage payment is not and should not be construed as a purchase price of the woman. She is not a commodity displayed for sale and she is not disadvantaged because of it. "2

Traditional African marriages were not based on romantic love; most marriages were arranged by the kinfolk, and families and were polygamous in nature. This meant that a man, if he wished and was able to provide for more than one wife, could marry more than one woman. With formal education and evangelization, however, modern women in traditional Africa are having a new look at a few of these rules, seeing them mainly as a means of keeping them down.

> The educated and trained women should take it upon themselves to do more than just struggle for better status for women. This status is a myth to the women who do not know what the law provides for their men. Most of our women are still very much ill-informed, the majority of our women are overburdened with chores that attempt to destroy life. A woman therefore has to educate the men to understand the harm done to society by its present imbalances and distorted images. She must train herself continuously to think, talk and act like a human being and not like some living tool called woman. 3

Today people are giving special emphasis to the women's liberation movement--a movement that has prompted the idea that women can do all that men can do and at times may do it better. African women have been able to distinguish themselves as political animals despite men's attitudes of superiority.

> The history books tell us that Ashanti women founded small states such as Mampong, Wenchi, and Juaben. These, however, are a matrilineal people, which may provide a possible explanation, although no such interpretation of them serves to explain that, on the west coast, and in the Cameroons

and the Congo region, even patrilineal groups would trace their genealogies back to eponymous ancestresses. [4]

Before the colonial government Ashanti women in Ghana and southern Nigerian women ruled jointly with the men. The arrival of the foreign rulers after 1885 brought the suppression of women in many parts of Africa. The structure of the administration was so arranged that women leaders were coopted to help the absolute monarchs in the day-to-day operation of the state. It was not common to see women as absolute rulers, but most of the African leaders then had many influential women around them who represented the interests of the women.

In the ancient kingdom of Benin in the midwestern part of Nigeria, it was the practice for the ruling monarch, three years after his ascension to the throne, to confer on his own mother the title of Iyoba (Queen's mother), after which she was then sent to Uselu, a part of the kingdom, to reign as Iyoba of Uselu and become one of the king's most important advisers until her death. [5]

To the west of the River Niger the Igbo culture allowed for two parallel rulers. In the kingdom of Obi there was a place for a female counterpart ruler, the Omu. The duty of the Omu was to see about the welfare of the women in the community. The ruler, Obi, is a hereditary successor to his clan's throne. Both the Obi and the Omu worked together for the betterment of their subjects. "In the kingdom of Oyo, a group of eight women of the highest class were known as the ladies of the palace. They were not the king's wives but resided in the palace with him as heads of small compounds within the palace walls. [6]

The above shows that African women were involved in politics before the arrival of the colonial government. It is a fact that the colonial rule suppressed women's power in Africa. By 1885 women's power was regarded as mob action. From Nigeria we could draw references as to how the colonial rule tried to eliminate women from politics. "In the kingdom of Benin the British Administration in 1889 abolished the post of Iyoba of Uselu which was begun in 1506. "[7]

Although the female institution of Omu was not formally abolished among the Igbo of western Nigeria, its existence was conveniently ignored by the colonial administration and in the reforms that swept through the country in the thirties, no mention was made of the Omu or her role. Only one monarch (Obi) was recognised and paid a salary. [8]

In the Igbo areas of eastern Nigeria democracy was practiced by consultation and consensus. When the colonial government arrived it could not understand the culture and traditions of the people it ruled. Without a thorough study the colonial administration proceeded to make laws without consulting the people of eastern Nigeria. As mentioned in the previous chapter, during the year 1926 the colonial administration imposed a tax system based on levy of the men. When a similar head count of the women was made in 1929, they reacted adversely and vehemently opposed the counting. They felt that if they were allowed to be counted, such action might result in their paying tax like the men. Such action by the colonial government was regarded as improper and a rape of justice--a foreign rule without proper consultation.

Most women from the old eastern provinces organized themselves in mass demonstrations in 1929. With palm fronds in their hands, they protested against the colonial rule and suppression of women. This was the first mass rally ever staged by women in colonial Africa. However, the colonial government did not tolerate this action from the women. They moved their soldiers in and shot thirty-two of the women and wounded thirty. From this date women were shut out of active politics.

> The effect was to muzzle women all around, to relegate them to the background, and to shut them out of active politics for a long time. On the national level, in the legislative councils of the colonial government, there is no record of a single woman appointed to represent her country in any of these government bodies throughout the colonial period. [9]

"In accordance we herewith appeal to all women in the world to unite with us and fight for peace, against all oppression and violation of our rights. "[10]

In colonial Africa education was established mainly for males; women were usually discriminated against. The aim of the educational policies of the colonial administration was

to produce not scholars, but clerical staff and interpreters
for the regime.   Only men could fulfill the task of keeping
the colonial administration supplied with cheap labor.   When
the girls' schools were built they were geared toward homemaking curricula--house crafts were the main subjects.   The
hard subjects, such as science and politics, were for men,
who would need education to have the power to rule.

> Everything was calculated to make the African girl
> the western idealized form of the home-bound and
> dependent wife and mother.   She was not to bother
> herself with the hard things of life....   The Chris-
> tian missionary activities which either preceded or
> accompanied colonial rule simply perpetrated the
> western ideal of the innate superiority of the men
> and, by implication, the inferiority of the women.
> Through their alien biblical teachings and their
> women's training programs, they stressed the obe-
> dient and dutiful wife-and-mother roles. [11]

The type of education available to men gave them the
push to search for a paying job in an urban setting, while
the wife's dependence increased as she followed her husband
to the urban areas, leaving farming behind.   As all the urban jobs were for men, the women then turned to retail trading in order to stay fully employed.   Taking what small
amount of cash she could get her hands on, she engaged in
petty trading.   A fraction of the woman represented foreign
firms in the open market, and a few of them became very
rich.   They bought with cash and also hoarded the profits.
The colonial agents often nicknamed them "merchant queens"
or "big market mammies. "

The post-Independence period was truly a period of
educational advancement.   Many newly independent African
countries increased their educational budgets tenfold.   The
discriminatory educational policy of the colonial administration was now replaced by different types of women's institutions.   At present women are competing very favorably with
their male counterparts for scholarships.   They are now
found in all phases of academic disciplines--law, medicine,
architecture, education, business, and top-level civil service.

In both the elementary- and secondary-school class-
rooms women sit side by side with men.   They march to
and from classes holding hands and usually sing the popular
children's song:

> "We are marching to our classes
> With clean hands and faces. "

Coeducation in Africa has made marriage by love possible for many women. Some meet their future spouses in school. The traditional (arranged) marriage is generally frowned upon. Women are competing strongly with their male counterparts--an opportunity that was rare during the colonial era. There are many changes sweeping Africa, but patterns of traditional life in the rural areas are still common, as women everywhere continue to admire the continuity of the traditional life. "We like our culture, particularly the bride price, " they say.

We have already noted that the colonial era did not favor the African women. They were discriminated against, disregarded, and at times force was used to subdue them. They became inactive in day-to-day politics. The postcolonial period, however, has seen African women joining the political parties of their choice. But they still wish for the politics of the precolonial times, when women ruled equally with men. The Independence era gave them the privilege of campaigning and marshaling the market women's votes, but after election, what? Most of the time women were not included in the national arena. At times they were so frustrated that they lost all confidence in national politics. When one considers the population of women in Africa, which is greater than that of the men, one would surely say that the sexual representation of the legislature should conform to that of the demographic situation.

Women's development in Africa may be defined as gradual evolution in the full use of women's potential in development efforts. Many people in the world see development as:

1. Growth in terms of per capita income.
2. Improvement in living income.
3. Ability to grow at one's own pace.
4. Eradication of hunger and malnutrition.
5. Development to be equated with economic growth.

Women's liberation slogans often revolve around the numbers of women in policy-making positions.

> The society, the state, and the public institutions
> all have a great responsibility for the development

of the family. In all its different forms, it makes
a special contribution to the development of the
human personality, in particular regarding the new
conditions for women. The parents are together
equally responsible for their children's physical and
mental development. Equality permits women to
decide by their own will whether to marry or not
and to marry men of their own choice. It permits
a harmonious division of labor between the husband
and wife in the family and it founds the base for
the development of skills of the two spouses in accordance with their interests. [12]

A few governments of the Third World have started to
recognize the importance of nutritional education for the rural women. African women must not only play the traditional
roles associated with cultural continuity, but are faced with
the challenge of a new one. "Expanding the social, political,
occupational and economic opportunities of women beyond the
traditional roles of motherhood and housekeeping enables them
to experience directly the advantages of lowered fertility and
channel their creative abilities over a much broader spectrum
of choice.... Governments should try above all else to raise
the status of women socially, economically and politically. "[13]

The flames that ignited in 1975 at the International
Women's Conference show that the divisions between the haves
and have-nots are still fresh in our memories. The priority
for African women has been more in the way of economic
betterment than of liberation. Those women who attended the
conference were a few privileged ones--the market groups
who form the pivots of the women's movement in Africa.
Market women's organizations may not be as strong and as
vocal as they used to be, but they are still the base and
rays of hope for the entire mass of peasant women. The
"new Eve" is anxious to get a piece of the modern pie, which
involves letting each society acknowledge her worth and role
in the development process. More and more, the stride is
quickening. Many African women are now members of the
Cabinet (Ministers of State), lawyers, writers, ambassadors,
and philanthropists of international stature.

Chapter 5

WOMEN'S MIGRATION AND PRODUCTION

Women's place was formerly said to be at home. At this
time, however, due to the women's liberation movement,
this adage may be reexamined. Formerly rural migrants
were mostly men who moved to the suburban and urban areas
to look for advancement through better jobs. This may be
called a commercial migration, which involves traders, job
seekers, and at times single women. There is also an in-
flux of teenagers leaving their rural homes for the cities,
whose ages range mainly from 18 to 21 years. Teenage
migration in Ghana, Nigeria, and Ivory Coast is very common. At times the teenagers are in the company of their
parents. From the precolonial period men have been migrat-
ing from their homes to the coastal regions for the trade.
Short migrations were made by the women of West Africa,
while the men migrated and remained for trade until they
retired from active business. "The Hausa, Duoula, and
Yorubas seem to have the longest histories of involvement
in trans-West African trade. They are probably the most
widely dispersed of the contemporary commercial migrants."[1]

"The Igbo who had well-developed internal trading net-
works in pre-colonial times but were not prominent in trans-
West African trade amplify the group who gained prominence
as commercial migrants in the twentieth century. "[2]

There are many Ghanaian women traders in Nigeria.
But Nigerian migrant women traders by far outnumber the
Ghanaians who are in Nigeria.   Most of the Nigerian women
traders in Ghana are Igbos.   They are mainly seen at Accra,
Takorodi, and Kumasi doing petty trading.   The female Yoruba migrants far outnumber the male Yorubas in the migrant
West African trade.   "At the time of the census,   70 per cent
of the adult Yoruba female population was reported as being
employed.   Of this 91 per cent were traders and another 7
per cent were self-employed in crafts and service occupations. "[3]

On the other hand, among the Hausa the males are
the international traders, and other self-employed workers
out-number their female counterparts by three to one.   In
fact, most Hausa women, due to seclusion in accordance with
their Moslem laws and traditions, are not recorded.

> Yoruba women constituted 44 per cent of the adult
> Yoruba population in Ghana; Hausa women only 33
> per cent of the adult population.   Other mobile
> female trading populations as shown by my research
> of migrating populations in Ghana include the Ewe
> of Togo, the Igbos of Nigeria, and various other
> ethnic groups from southern Nigeria.   In fact,
> southern Nigerian women including the Yoruba and
> the Igbos appear to have been the largest group
> of female international migrants in West Africa.[4]

As we recorded in the previous chapters, the goal of
many African women is economic betterment.   In the modern
era more women have left the rural farms for the urban
areas in search of a better life.   A few of them who still
dwell on the rural farms are no longer looking at farming
as a supplementary enterprise.   They soon change to urban
migratory work or perform piece work, which in the short
run brings quicker returns.   Early in the morning many of
the farm women take taxis to the urban centers to work and
then return back to their rural homes at the end of the day.
In this way the agricultural labor force suffers greatly because of the lack of workers.   Does this represent a shift
from the rural to the urban setting, which was traditionally

a man's way of life? Wage employment is drawing more women from agricultural labor. Despite world inflation, the
food supply is short, thereby forcing prices up in the market.

> Three-quarters of the male N. T. C. employees are
> married and live with their wives. These workers
> are linked through their wives to the indigenous
> economy; in complementary fashion, through mar-
> riage to factory employees, women from diverse
> backgrounds are part of the small Zaria working
> class. The households of the permanent workers
> at N. T. C. are economically secure in comparison
> with these small scale businessmen and traders and
> the main source of income is the husband's wage
> packet. Only one of the twenty-four women inter-
> viewed was wage-employed herself; the remainder
> either hoped to be or were active in the Zaria in-
> digenous economy. [5]

Though women's work was lighter, it continued year
around. Women participated in planting, collecting and harvesting crops, in addition to transporting them home. They
also helped men to clear grass, weeds ... women cultivated
their small millet fields, to be used for additional food. [6]

Farm labor is one of the most important forces of
peasant agriculture. When a farmer talks of supplying labor
he or she means the amount of work that can be done in a
given time. A family harvesting an acre of yams first must
dig the yams out of the ground, transfer them into baskets,
and then haul them to the barns for storage. In any economic production labor is used to make things more useful by
changing their farms, location, or their time of consumption.
For instance, let's have a look at how farmers and their families expand their labor from the period when rice is planted
until it is harvested.

The first step is to plough the ground with a hoe,
then the rice is planted, picked, and threshed. Finally the
rice is hauled, usually on the head, to the market. In this
simple model both capital and labor have been involved. The
farmer uses two important forms of labor on the farm throughout the year: family labor and hired or cooperative labor.
The farm labor is divided among the husband, the wife, and
the children. There are certain areas of labor allotted entirely to the father. This type of labor is more physical in

rticularly in West Africa the palm nut has be[en a]
[m]ajor cash crop. At present the introduction o[f]
[ne]w rehabilitation programs is still in its infancy.
[Colle]cting and processing of wild palm nuts are gene[rally]
[the work] of women and children. They go around the fo[rest]
[collecting] overripe palm nuts that have dropped from the [trees.]
The work of climbing the trees and cutting down t[he bunch]
containing the nuts is done by the men.

When enough palm nuts have been collected and pro[cessed,]
and the oil extracted, they are left to dry before
[th]e cracked for kernels. These processes require che[mical]
[oil] and that comes from women and children. Palm pro[duce]
[h]as been a major cash crop in Africa, and a source
[fore]ign exchange earnings. In southern Nigeria and other
[Africa]n countries large wild palm groves may be seen in the
[region] but now different domestic varieties are grown on the
[planta]tion farms.

Currens studies the subsistence production among the
[Loma] of Liberia, and his findings concerned the migrants
[th]e rice farms and the use of hired labor. He found that

it is significant that up to the present no Loma
citizen of Lawalazu will accept employment for
money on any other citizen's rice farm or for
other agricultural work; strangers are the only
ones who can be hired. Citizens fall into the
category of kin or friend and their labor can be
enlisted by a farmer on the basis of traditional
patterns of generalized reciprocity, specific kin,
the obligations incumbent upon relatives to give
assistance.10

In his pioneering study on migrant labor Currens
[fo]und that "other factors have contributed to the increase
[in] personal farms--relationships among household members,
[th]e availability of labor for hire, and new techniques for
[g]rowing rice in inundated areas."11

Loafing on the job is an attempt to slow down the production in order to stay longer on the job. The way to check
the labor deficit seems to be to let the hired worker take
the job in the form of piecework or by cooperative exchange
of labor. As one farmer put it, "If Nwaokorabia [young man]
relaxes on my farm, I will advise my own family to relax on
his as well." The owner of the farm and his hired man make

---

nature--cutting the bush, tilling the soil, staking of yams,
digging, and harvesting. The less physical type of labor is
reserved for the women and children, although women's work
is a continuous routine, day in and day out, year in and year
out, during both dry periods and rainy seasons. Tilling, digging, and delving, and other work on the farm, as well as
transportation of the crop, are the activities allotted mainly
to the women.

Baumann (1928) conducted an extensive survey of the
division of labor by sex in African hoe culture. Hoe culture
refers to a farming system in which the hoe constitutes the
major technology used on the farms. This includes eastern,
central, and southern Africa. Baumann observed that in such
a system of subsistence agriculture men's labor input on the
farms consisted of clearing bush before the land was dug.
It was confined to a short period, whereas work done by women continued throughout the agricultural year. He noted
that women were in charge of growing the oldest root crops,
kitchen vegetables, and spices. They also tended to intro-
duce new food crops. He cited one instance that indicated
that division of labor on the farm and in the household made
men largely dependent on women as providers of food. 7

As more women and youth leave the farm to enter
educational institutions, they leave behind their house and
farm chores, thereby reducing the amount of family labor
available. The farmer and his family often work more than
eight hours a day during the period of planting and harvesting. After selecting the type of crop to grow the farmer can
then calculate the number of days of work involved and the
amount of help needed, excluding the family labor. During
the off season, when the activities are fewer on the farm,
the farmer takes up other jobs around the house, such as
repairing fences, tidying around the buildings, and checking
for proper drainage. The farmer's wife is busy every min-
ute of the day. When the farm work is over, she works
around her vegetable garden at home. She must check on
crops like peppers and tomatoes, and in addition prepare
meals for the household. After the evening meals, during
the dry season when water is most scarce, she carries a
four-gallon container on her head and goes to a nearby stream
or river to draw water.

"African women have been active in the provisioning
of their families. This is the role which they play today although they are being constricted in their efforts to feed their

families by multinational corporations in food processing and
agribusiness as well as by national land reform and crop pr
grams."8   Labor distribution varies at different periods of
the year.   A few crops are planted at different times and
also harvested in different seasons of the year.   In the southern regions yams are planted in February.   The busiest of
all months for farm work are June and July, when weeds
must be kept under control.   The work is not done by me-
chanical means, but by hand and sometimes with a hoe.   This
type of job is reserved primarily for women and children.
The activities of farming commence immediately after the
first rain has moistened the ground.   The planted crops remain on the farm until the harvest period, which is usually
accompanied by joy and happiness as the year's harvest boun-
ty is celebrated.

     To clearly show the part played by women on the
farm we may calculate the number of man-days and woman-
days.   During the peak period, it is estimated that man-days
and woman-days are 46 and 39 respectively in the months of
June and July.   Phillip (1961) stated that most of the task
is performed in June and July, when the labor on the farm
reaches its peak.

     Jan Wills in a 1967 study of the Embu of Kenya
noted the description of the pre-colonial division
of labor between the sexes in Embu society, re-
sulting mainly from the high male absenteeism from
the countryside.   Consequently, women had to perform men's work in order to fill the gap.   That
the reverse is uncommon implies that women increasingly made more production and marketing
decisions and contributed more physical labor.   In
Zambia and Malawi, for instance, 30-50 per cent
of able-bodied men worked outside their home area.
In 1940, it was found that in Kabwe (formerly Broken Hill), Zambia, 69.9 per cent of the African
labor force (6,460 men) had spent two-thirds of
their time in town since leaving their homes....
     In Kabwe, the African male population of 7,500
had with it a total female population of 3,500 and
4,000 children.   For every dependent present, three
remained in the rural areas.   However, urban
dwellers consumed nine tenths of their cash wages
in town including in-kind remuneration.   Thus the
countryside was clearly exploited by the towns.
Furthermore, most of the men in town were young

(average age in Kabwe
often having left the co
under 16 years.8

As the peak period in most Africa
and August, the farmer may hire
when one or two of the family mem
My survey in the rural farm areas
tablished that a farm with two adults
work 300 days annually.9   The additi
the form of cooperative exchange gro
migratory labor, mostly hoe women,
bor.   These laborers receive about th
full work, while skilled labor receives
plus lunch and dinner.   However, this
country to another.

     From the above it can be seen th
required in order to get workers from o
to another.   Most skilled farm jobs are
Good workers are usually employed year-r
deserve steady jobs and could find year-ro
elsewhere.   It is very difficult for the wo
unskilled male labor when their husbands ta
jobs.   With the idea that at the end of the
skilled and casual laborers will be paid, the
for these groups of farm workers to relax o
sary breaks in the palm-grove shade, particu
woman owner is out of sight.

     A few farms--mainly those that grow c
processing equipment.   Rice cultivation is a ca
that needs women's and children's labor.   Wher
of rice are planted and harvested, a large porti
ly's labor--which should have been applied to so
like cocoa and coffee--is diminished.   Where the
are grown, women generally pick the crops.   Co
runs from September until January, while coffee
from November until January.

     Another cash crop cultivated mainly by the
peanuts.   Peanuts are cultivated in early April and
early June.   The July-to-August peanut harvest is a
work of the women.   After the peanuts are harvested
are dried immediately so as not to allow them to ger
The nuts are washed, dried, and shelled, and are the
for the export-trade market.

come a
palm-gro
The colle
the work
collectin
trees.
bunches

cessed,
they a
labor,
duce h
of for
Africa
forest
planta

Loma
on th

an oral agreement, specifying the quantity of work to be done each day. This may be the best way the farmer can induce honorable work and high worker productivity.

The farmer's reason for hiring outside labor is to see that the work is done on time; if some activities are delayed, yield may be reduced. It is vitally important to plant immediately after the rainfall--as soon as the ground is moistened--and to weed to avoid competition of weeds with crops. To delay this will definitely retard crop growth. To finish the work the farmer should hire additional hands; an additional hand would increase output per acre, thus increasing farm efficiency. Although the female peasant farmer is not usually schooled in the scientific methods of farming, she has been on the farm long enough to acquire knowledge of the necessary operations required to run it.

If a farmer wants to make a good profit from her operation, she must devote her time to the more important decisions that will have more bearing on her profits. If she needs more yams from the harvest, she must increase her efficiency which in turn will increase output for labor expended. Any profit realized from the farm depends on sales of different commodities produced on the farm. If the prevailing wage is three dollars per day, then it is advisable to raise crops to cover the amount, with a few dollars left over. But if the wage rises to six dollars per day per person, it would be unprofitable to do the same things as when the wage was three dollars. To break even the farmer may increase his or her daily operation. However, African farmers are very strict when hiring additional labor, as the extended family has been very useful in supplying a major part of the labor for the farm.

The farmers are concerned not with the scarcity of labor but with the problem of which job is to be done or left undone at prevailing farm prices and wage levels. On most farms the farmer and his family do the greater proportion of the labor, because hiring extra labor may involve the problem of keeping the extra hands employed during the slack seasons. On many farms a little more than 75 percent of the labor is done by the farmer himself, with about 15 percent by a hired hand and the rest by the farmer's family. The unpaid family labor is considered at the going hired wage rate.

The preponderance of women in the rural areas of

of Kenya has long been recognized.   In the 1969 Kenya census 1.7 million rural households were enumerated with an
adult population of 4.4 million and a female majority of 2.3
million.   It was further indicated that of the total 1,938,186
households in the urban and rural areas 571,385 had females
as heads of households.   Of the households with female heads
only 46,029 were to be found in urban centers with popula-
tions of 2,000 or more, so that at least 525,000 households
in the rural areas of Kenya were headed by women. [12]

The household may be made up primarily of a woman
and her children, especially when the man works.   Often
early in the morning the women rise before other members
of the family to clean around the compound and prepare break-
fast for the children.   Sometimes they have to go to the
stream to draw water for drinking before doing the normal
chores.   There are many chores that are never recorded by
women.   They regard such labors as primary duties of running a household.   Pala notes a table that

> presents data on time allocation by women accord-
> ing to different tasks, and what is significant in
> the table is that in both dry and wet seasons pre-
> paration of meals alone requires more time than
> other activities (15.1 mean hours in dry season;
> 12.7 mean hours in wet season per week).   Food
> and cash crops take 10.8 and 14.1 mean hours
> per week in the wet season respectively.   Fetching
> water takes 1.9 mean hours in the wet season and
> 3.6 hours per week in the dry season. [13]

Pala, in his research in Kenya's Kisumu district,
shows that the average household is comprised of a woman
and her children.   The woman spends the first two hours
before sunrise (i.e., 5 to 7 a.m.), two hours around mid-
day (12 noon to 2 p.m.), and four hours after sunset (6 to
10 p.m.) every day on domestic work.   Fetching wood takes
from five to ten hours per week, since distances to wooded
areas where firewood can be found increase as the villagers
cut further back into the forest.   Most women devote between
two and five hours a week to community affairs.   This includes churchgoing and attending self-help project meetings,
which are normally held for an additional two or three hours
after the church services.

The question is, how could women's labor be lessened,
so that more of their time could be used to greater advantage?

If all the women owned bicycles, most of their errands could
be done easily, as faster transportation would reduce the time
involved in trekking to the distant markets. If the government would provide the communities with drinking wells or
piped water, then women in the rural areas could save time
and energy expended in going to the streams and rivers to
fetch water. The rural farm could have a new look by using
intercropping methods, such as alternating yams with cassava.
Such reorganization of farms would surely eliminate excess
labor for all family members.

Chapter 6

WOMEN'S SELF-HELP AND COOPERATION

In Africa there are many different cooperatives, but the cooperatives that could provide the avenues for women to market their produce are still in their infancy. A few credit societies are still not well-enough developed to render good
services to women members.

With the growing competition in trade and marketing
and the increase in the cost of living, the need for women's
cooperative societies becomes even greater. It is a fact
that African farming methods are very primitive in compari-
son with those in more advanced countries. The ways of doing most productive things are very poor, especially in the
marketing system. Most of the African peasant women have
no capital; therefore in order to produce more food women
must borrow from their neighbors or money lenders. Women's associations may not be able to get credit from a commercial bank, as men can. Banks traditionally make no
loans to them because of their position in African society.
Peasants do not always represent good risks and therefore

the commercial banks make practically no loans to their organizations. "The investigation showed that there was an appalling lack of credit facilities available to farmers as well as farmers' cooperative societies. The principal sources of the limited credit were the cooperative thrift and credit societies."[1] If the women in Africa, especially the market women, are to make rapid progress in the rural areas of their respective countries, they must create new conditions so as to get assistance from both the government and the commercial banks for their organizations (see Appendix).

In Africa the social norms of the people are based on a tradition of mutual help and cooperation. The women's groups need to organize their own cooperatives, which will enable governments to channel assistance to women farmers-- be it financial, technical, educational, or otherwise. The cooperative may be the only easy way that women's organizations can meet their business obligations.

In the rural areas of all African countries the exorbitant rate of interest charged by the moneylenders and the exploitation of the consumers by high prices necessitate the formation of women's cooperatives. The inability of the farm women to realize a fair price on their commodities due to lack of organization and marketing information in the local areas makes the formation of cooperatives, for food, credit, marketing, handicrafts, in the rural farm areas essential. Cooperatives will help restore and retain the freedom of the individual through self-organization. The ideal of the women's combined efforts in their different organizations will no doubt be displayed on the rural farms, which in turn will encourage and develop the practical application of democratic methods for the economic works of the community. Hon. Dr. Ogbonna, former minister in charge of cooperatives in eastern Nigeria, puts it thus: "Cooperative society is a voluntary and democratic organization of persons who organize themselves to improve or consolidate their individual economic or social needs by mutual action." Several aspects of this definition deserve full attention. First, a cooperative is a device that permits group actions for the economic gains of the individual members. There are many good things that women and farm producers could accomplish by working with their neighbors or by exchanging their laborers, which economically they could not do alone. During the peak season or the planting season, when much labor is required on the farm, the women farmers could then exchange laborers.

The growth of the cooperative movement in some African countries has been remarkable and has made much progress, but only a few could be associated with women to provide an avenue for them to increase their food crops, so that a surplus could be sold in the market. Because many women are engaged in petty trading, craftsmen's cooperatives, consumers' cooperatives, and thrift and loan societies could be developed and operated primarily for these women. In Africa many cooperatives have developed, but none operates entirely for women. The few existing cooperatives may cater both to the interests of men and women, but men are always in control of the groups.

Craftsmen's Cooperatives

This type of cooperative should be developed with due safeguards where the people demand them; particular care should be taken to avoid mutual conflicts and competition among societies. Since the danger of competition among societies is ever-present, such cooperatives should, where possible, operate under a parent organization that will influence and control, within national limits, the disposal of the products of any particular type. This will provide a means of regulating production of the class of goods required by the market, which in turn will ensure the best overall marketing results and will maintain standards of quality and design.

Consumers' Cooperatives

The policy with regard to establishment of cooperative retail shops should be one of caution; although there is no objection to the adoption of a progressive policy when the demand originates from the people themselves, and where they are prepared to find their own capital and to accept the full risk. Such organizations cannot, however, expect either direct or indirect subsidies from the government, and must make their own arrangements to produce their supplies through such commercial channels as they think best. Shops established by such societies should, at least for the present, confine their trading activities to members.

Thrift and Loan Societies

A steady expansion of this type of society with a view to en-

able members to make regular savings for their retirement
years, to make deposits in special savings for special objectives, and to obtain loans against their savings to meet
unforeseen expenses, should be encouraged.

Women farmers should band themselves together in the
marketing of their domestic crops--yams, cassava, millet,
bananas, coco-yams, sweet potatoes, guinea corn, and cow
peas. Their cash crops are sold primarily through European
merchants or cooperative marketing societies consisting mostly
of men--who have banded together in cooperatives--while their
crops for domestic consumption are taken to the local or
wholesale markets.

> Farmers and peasants in many parts of the world
> are either without organizations or the existing or-
> ganizations are ineffective agents of the farms in
> either the political or the economic sense. In the
> United States, however, the farmers' organizations
> are structurally complex and play significant econo-
> mic, political and social roles in the lives of Ameri-
> can farmers.[2]

> I saw another example of community development
> in Awu-Mama in Orlu Division of the eastern region
> of Nigeria, which was carried on mostly in the
> sphere of social and cultural life, but with signifi-
> cant beginnings in the economic field and it was
> very successful. The problems which arise when
> the organization in the economic life of the village
> is to be established are far more complex and diffi-
> cult to handle and to solve than the ones that social
> and cultural matters deal with, like health, and edu-
> cation, because economic matters are mostly inter-
> connected with and affected by social conditions.[3]

Women's Credits

There are many economic associations that include the members of the kinship groups, but are not operated on kinship
principles. Most operate either with an oral-contract agreement or a written agreement. Most of these associations
open their membership to males, but at times there are many
who limit membership to their peer groups and professionals.
The qualification for entry into a few of these associations is
the ability of an interested individual to be able to meet the

terms of the agreement. Some terms of the agreement may
limit the entry of women because of their status.

In Africa there are many nonkinship associations operating, such as work groups, native doctors' associations
(herbalist, diviner, and medicine man), and credits. The
most common of all of these associations is the cooperative
exchange group, usually organized in the community when
labor is scarce or the job on the farm has reached its peak.
It is a common belief on the rural farms that hiring of outside labor is a waste of available money, as any deficit in
the labor supply could be made up by the family. Since the
woman farmer is unable to pay additional labor, she generally
favors the use of cooperative labor as a source of making up
the labor deficit on her farm, especially during the periods
of planting, weeding, and harvesting of the crops.

> Wagner argued that economic cooperation among
> family members in the Kitosha and Maragoli com-
> munities of the Baluyia was important. It was en-
> couraged by the insignificant exchange value and
> short-lived utility of goods, resulting from low
> level technology and a general undifferentiated ec-
> onomy with little exhange of goods.
> In addition to hoeing, women cooked, carried
> water and wood, gathered wild roots and vegetables,
> and ground sorghum. Both men and women joined
> in planting, weeding, and harvesting. Consequently,
> the family was a self-sufficient economic unit with
> its members working in a complementary fashion. [4]

While many of these associations are vital to women
and farm groups, petty credit institutions or women's organizations provide the farmer or trader with ready cash during
the peak seasons. There are many petty credit systems
operating in different parts of Africa. Before the arrival
of European colonialists many of these credit associations
existed in more primitive forms. The early period of credit came with the arrival of money lenders and high rates
of interest charged, and also through the institution of cre-
dit-pawning. The elders or the family heads started to pawn
their palm trees, rubber trees and orange trees when there
was great need for immediate cash.

The institution of credit is similar to a credit union
or savings club. A group of individuals makes a specific
contribution of money at a fixed time, such as every Sunday

or market day.   The total amount contributed each period is
assigned to one of the members in rotation.   The number of
contributions is limited to about twenty or fewer persons, and
the length of time for the contribution varies from group to
group.   The "Isusu" equation runs in this way: each person
pays a fixed amount of one dollar per month, and for twenty
months he or she will receive twenty dollars at his or her
turn in the cycle.   There is no gain or loss in this association, but each member has a lump sum with which to buy
more yams, repay accumulated debts, and pay school fees
for children.   An attempt is always made to make the funds
available to members in times of great need.   Often, due
to internal rivalry, a member who applies for the contribution at a time when he or she is in need may be disappointed
unless he or she is quite clever.   The thrift and primitive
credit societies were based partly on the principles of the
indigenous loan club of Isusu.   With the Isusu club, members
contribute regularly and the total amount collected is paid
to each member in turn.   It is a useful way for the women's
organizations to save and to realize capital for their needs.
However, abuses often creep into the Isusu club.   A default-
ing member who fails to make a contribution on time may
lose all the payments previously made.   Members could ac-
cumulate their savings and buy goods on credit.   Their membership is sufficient to guarantee short-term or long-term
credit from local moneylenders.   When a member of Isusu
is unable to pay his or her debt after taking a share, that
member may desert or migrate.

        The club meets once a week in the marketplace on
market day or after Sunday services.   The chairlady of the
group conducts business in one of the market huts or in an
empty classroom.   The recipient of the monthly contribution
signs the book or makes a thumb print.   In many areas when
one gets a hand (share), one pays about 5 percent of the take-
out to the women's organization, which is reserved in the
club treasury and used for emergency loans to the members.

            The weakness of the Isusu is that the members
            do not always get the money when they need it.
            One member gets his "hands" [turn] on it when he
            could do without it, while another may be desper-
            ately in need of money but cannot get anything be-
            cause it is not his turn. [5]

        The Isusu club seems to give too much power to the
chairwoman, who at times abuses the power delegated to her

by the organization by not considering those members who
are in great need.

Credit Club

This type of credit institution formed by the so-called professional women draws its membership from students, teachers and government and local-council employees. The members pay a very high rate of contribution every month; take-
out is once every year. Membership is not limited and is
open to both men and women. For the government and local council employees, from a dollar to five dollars is deducted from their salary each month (pay as you earn). Petty traders, tinkers, and drivers pay five dollars per month.
Members do not take a loan from their treasury as in other
associations; the idea is to see that the members save. With
their take-outs, members can take land lease, become village
moneylenders, provide second burial ceremonies for their
deceased parents, or buy new bicycles. In addition, men
can make a bride-price payment. Often members use their
take-outs to buy a bicycle for work or purchase a new sewing machine. Unlike other credit institutions, members do
not give a party or a feast during the take-outs. A member
of this club may sign over his or her rights to a take-out in
order to borrow cash, raise trading capital, or buy goods on
credit.

    In the Yoruba land of western Nigeria credit was
available to the farmers and petty traders at a high interest
rate. Many farmers pawned their cocoa trees in order to
obtain some credit for other things. Credit is now also
available through the institution of "Esusu." In this club
each person pays a fixed fee for a prescribed period of time,
and the funds are added together and given to one member
at a time. Each member of the Esusu club gets this fund
in rotation. The nature and size of contributions vary according to the groups. One group may prefer that contributions be made each week and assigned to each member weekly,
while other groups may prefer the monthly contribution. If
one member contributes thirty dollars, he or she also receives thirty dollars in return. The advantage is that the
member may not be able to save up to thirty dollars on his
or her own, and by paying a bit at a time, he or she would
be able to save enough in the form of contributions to the
club.

The Esusu is a fund to which a group of individuals
make fixed contributions of money at fixed intervals; and the total amount contributed each period
is assigned to each of the members in rotation.
The number of contributions, the size of the contributions, and the length of the intervals between
contributions vary from one group to another; but
if twenty members contribute one shilling each
month, at the end of twenty months, which com-
pletes the cycle, each member will have contributed one pound, and will have received one pound
in return. [6]

Thrift and Savings

The cooperative thrift and savings societies are comprised mostly of salaried women who allow some percentage
of their salaries to be deducted.   There have been many difficulties in Africa--particularly in Nigeria--in establishing
this type of society due to spending habits.   The thrift and
credit societies were created to serve the interests of the
farmers and petty traders.   They were based partly on the
principles of cooperative credit and also on the principle
of the loan club of Isusu.

The cooperative credit society may be called a con-
tributory savings from the men and women members.   The
fees are fixed according to what the poorest members can
afford to pay.   There is also the lending of money to farmers
by brokers and moneylenders, who charge the farmers very
high interest rates because there is no bank of cooperation.
Because the farmers deal with the brokers and moneylenders,
they can scarcely fulfill their commitment to their respective
organizations.   This would indicate that moneylenders in general are not desirable sources of credit, since the rate of
interest charged is so high.   On a few occasions the dis-
honest lenders may force the farmers to sign documents to
double what they have actually received (i.e., a 100-percent
interest rate).   The lenders and brokers enjoy a financial
advantage at the expense of the farmers and market women.
They argue that the high interest charged is due to the fact
that most of the farmers and/or traders are great risks.
They further feel that due to uncertainty in agriculture the
lenders may not be sure of being paid at harvest time.   To
rectify some of the irregularities the system of cooperative
credits and thrift was introduced for the advantage of the

rural farmers. The cooperative credit societies then give
out loans to members from the accumulated share capital
of the societies. The rate of 15-percent interest is charged
per pound sterling ($3) in Nigeria.

African Women

The abovementioned 15-percent rate, however, is more
favorable than the rate given by moneylenders. The farm
and market women know that through good credit they may
change the course of their business and organizations. The
women surely would upset the middlemen who make excessive
profits in marketing channels, if they could organize their
cooperatives well. Hence these groups, the women's clubs,
thrift and savings and consumer cooperatives, will capture
most of the profits that otherwise would have gone to the
moneylenders, who tended to increase the returns to themselves.

Improvement of the level of living and increasing productivity are not only accepted social objectives in Africa,
but are economic necessities as well. The improvement of
women's programs over both long and short terms will give
women a position of decision making, although in most of
the cooperative groups studied women seemed to have the
least membership. "The extension services have tended to
exclude women or teach them things that do not enhance their
skills in agriculture. It is important to clarify here that
we are not interested in the role of women in the rural development simply because they are women."[7]

Chapter 7

RURAL DEVELOPMENT AND WOMEN

The experiences of African women in their struggle for economic development are similar to those of other women moving through social, political, and economic changes. The struggle to overcome obstacles that have created barriers to their economic and social emancipation is often in conflict with their traditional culture. In a recent and very important statement about politics in Algeria, Mohamed remarked that "the real ... wretched of the earth in Fanon's well-known phrase were the women of Africa, the most abused, the most exploited, the most in need of social, cultural and economic liberation."[1]

The most pressing problem for African women, besides the education of their children, is the increase of their subsistence production of agriculture, which in turn will increase their industrial production. When the income of the rural population increases, it will limit the number of women who plan to migrate to the urban areas for a better living. As women's work at home is never ended, so also the role

of women in the rural economies remains unfulfilled.   For
most women on the rural farms the great opportunity is still
a dream.   Women have often desired some technical training, but they are often neglected by the extension officers.
The input and output of the rural African women is an indi-
cation that they need more and better training in agricultural
production and marketing operations.   For them to achieve
good and profitable marketing better policies and programs
should be pursued for the benefit of the rural farmers.   Individual participation has been common among women themselves, but more cooperative participation is necessary in
development activities, as procedures and policies of imple-
menting the idea of new farm settlement and development do
not yet appear to be clearly understood.   The rival planners
and policymakers should make a long-range plan that will fit
into a new situation and improve the workers' social conditions.   This program will focus on building a more satisfy-
ing and rewarding way of life for the women of Africa and
their families.

       The farm women believe that agriculture should have
an equality of income with the nonagricultural sector of the
economy.   Obviously they are aware of the substantial concentration of economic power in the nonfarm economy, which
is often wielded to the disadvantage of the rural families.
A common sign of decline in agricultural prices and income
can be seen in the outcries of the producers of commodities
and also by the market women.   The pressing issues are
how to increase per-capita output and how the commodities
produced on the farms may move more rapidly from the
rural areas to the consumers.   The women farmers are ignorant of what happens along the marketing chain.   In most
African countries the marketing board or "Causa Destabilization" handles all the export commodities collected from the
farms at a fixed rate.   The distribution problems--namely
the prevailing prices in the world's markets--are why some
of these marketing agencies are operated, in order to control the output and market supplies during periods of fluctu-
ation.   While the marketing boards in different countries fix
the prices by law for the consumer and producer, there is
no attempt on the part of most of the marketing boards to
include market women in planning and agricultural policies.

       National policy is not made in such a way as to pro-
tect the women and other users of farm products.   The problems of rural planning are difficult enough, yet the government will do such disservice to its nation if it carelessly

permits emotions to blind it to the need for a more careful analysis of how best to bring every relevant bit of knowledge to its improvement.

Yudelman reviewing the economic conditions and prospects for African agricultural development in southern, central and east Africa, estimated that 95 percent of the crops and 60 percent of the livestock produced by Africans in South Africa did not enter the market; more than 85 percent of the value of African produce in Malawi, Zambia, and Rhodesia (then the Federation of Rhodesia and Nyasaland) was for subsistence; and at least 80 percent of the value of African production in east Africa did not enter the exchange economy.[2]

However, market-oriented trade in the pre-colonial period did not produce an economy integrated by the marketing principles. The farm women and their families continued to depend primarily on subsistence agriculture for their livelihoods. The production of vital foodstuffs was only marginally affected by the market demands. All societies were affected by market-oriented trade, but the changes were generally confined to a relatively restricted sector of an economy which remained predominantly one of subsistence agriculture until rail and motor transport arrived in the area of production to solve the early problem of bulk export.

The arrival of colonial rule exposed Africans to better organized traditional markets with overwhelming competition, but only a privileged few could benefit from such competition. The foreign tendency to development in the twentieth century virtually disregarded the interests of the women in agriculture. Even the post-colonial trade disregards and overrides the women's major economic initiatives. The assumption is that the policy makers of the post-colonial period have continued to ignore the basic problems of African women in agriculture.

"I am suggesting that the problems facing African women today, irrespective of their national and social class affiliations, are inextricably bound up in the wider struggle by African people to free themselves from poverty and ideological domination in both the intra- and international sphere."[3] The development of agriculture and markets should be the primary concern for all African governments. The problem of expanding and improving production per acre is most vital because it concerns the largest section of the population and the most important sector of the African economy.

African women are thirsty for the fruits of human labor that already exist in the developed world. They will
certainly reject an ideology that does not place in women a
true disposition for the things of this earth or that alienates
them in any way from the pursuit of technological improve-
ments of the material world. At the same time, they yearn
to preserve the values integral to their personal worth and
integrity. They have long experienced the dehumanization of
their person, the devaluation of their worth by different cultures. The refusal of males to consider them equal in the
same family has intensified their struggle for liberation. The
elites among them refuse to accept unequal partnership.

> Not equally so, of course in all societies as the
> vigorous tradition and practices of women traders
> and entrepreneurs in coastal West Africa (and not
> only there) is enough to prove. Yet it may well
> be these enterprising ladies are, in fact, the ex-
> ceptions which confirm the rule. What otherwise
> explains, even in West Africa, the still very great
> rarity of ladies who accede to political, adminis-
> trative, or other executive power? And is it not
> indeed the case to glance at another aspect of the
> evidence that the veiling of ladies (with all this
> implies for their scope as members of society) is
> not on the decline in some northern states in Ni-
> geria (for example) but actually on the increase. [4]

There are many difficult problems to be tackled besides ignorance and bad methods of production. Besides implements created by the land tenure, social and religious
conventions, habits, traditional attitudes toward the land and
manual work, one-crop cultivation, and low productivity, financial assistance for further improvement is urgently needed.
The position of women will not be improved if new techniques
are transferred piecemeal, but every transfer of a new technique implies change in several dimensions.

All the farm women throughout Africa have shown a
considerable response to economic incentives that will increase production. However, agricultural innovations that
reduce technical risks have not gained a precise and scientific understanding among the women. It is hoped that the
cooperative movements introduced into women's organizations
can play a substantial part in encouraging savings in good
years and granting credit in bad ones. Cooperative marketing may be encouraged by government aids and subsidies in

order to be able to store the members' commodities.   There
is a great need for technical skills.   African women are looking for technical and economic progress in farming and farm
products.   They are in great need of technical progress that
arises from the new knowledge of the soil, animal diseases,
pests, and implements and tools; economic progress in agriculture has required more than technical knowledge alone.
Directing extension services to the rural family will guarantee
many new benefits to African women.

Malnutrition, transportation problems, bad housing
and sanitation, and disease are some of the obstacles to rural progress.   Improvement in these areas is now long over-
due.   Development of credit programs, introduction of small
tractors and plows, made to fit well into peasant agriculture,
will have much impact.   The continued neglect of women in
rural development by the extension specialists all over Africa
seems to show that there is a bias for future growth of a
sound African economy.   The major aim of the extension
people should be to stress the importance of domestic production of agricultural consumer goods for the expansion of
local markets.

> As a result of the attitudes of the extension ser-
> vice, the gap between the labour productivity of
> men and women thus continues to widen.   Men
> are taught to apply modern methods in the cultiva-
> tion of a given crop, while women continue to use
> traditional methods in the cultivation of a given
> crop, thus getting much less output from their ef-
> forts than men.   The inevitable result is that wo-
> men are discouraged from participating in agricul-
> tural development and are glad to abandon cultiva-
> tion whenever their husbands' income makes it
> possible. [5]

Baumann has observed that women in African culture
are mostly responsible for food production, and Edels corro-
borated Baumann's observations.   "The division of labor
among the Chiga of western Uganda suggested that the entire
responsibility of agricultural production rested mostly with
women who turn the soil, sowed, weeded, and harvested."[6]
Despite the fact that disguised unemployment lingers around
the rural farm, there are fluctuations in yield especially during the period of harvest, when the commodities harvested
reach the market at the same time.   In the markets some
basic commodities are very high during the producing seasons,

and after the season. The main reasons for this are sum-
marized as follows:

1. The production per acre is very low.
2. The scarcity of such home crops in the market.
3. Sharp fluctuations in export crops may affect the producers' prices.
4. Crop failures during a series of bad seasons.

All over Africa historical conferences on women have
emphasized that there is no national development plan inimical
to women. It has recently become an axiom that women are
the main source of production and marketing of foods in Africa. But the question remains whether women's food production ever kept pace with African population so as to produce enough food for the export market. What women often
discuss in their organizations is how the economy can provide the increasing population with a modern standard of
living. The problem of supplying adequate food and well-
balanced meals presents a definite challenge to women and
children.

The marketing margin between the producers and the
world market is so large that as a result the women producers usually receive a lower price for their crops than
do men. It is certain that the rural farmers are not expect-
ing the prices that are prevailing in the world market, nor
are they seeking to equalize the substantial concentrations
of economic power in the nonfarm economy, which are often
wielded to the disadvantage of women. African women have
clearly understood the loss of potential in their role in rural
development for decades. To breach the gaps that have existed between men and women the most pressing need now
is to increase production and thereby receive a fair price to
enable women to meet their national and international com-
mitments. It has been substantially proven that, despite all
claims, women are keys to agricultural production and
distribtuion for domestic consumption. Inadequate food programs are no longer rated as news. To increase per-capita
income on the rural farm the agricultural planners should reinforce the popular statements from the nonfarm groups, who
often have the feeling that it is necessary to have agricultural
prosperity in order to maintain national economic prosperity.

African women have no land rights. Their culture does
not allow them to dispose of any piece of land, although they
could use the land for the production of food, by the virtue

of being a wife, sister, daughter, or cousin. Surely land-
lessness of women brings insecurity and uncertainty in the
production of agriculture and availability of food. Could
such land tenure be changed to favor the women? The statu-
tory land rights in many African countries do not favor women, while at the same time they agree with the customary
laws in letting the male dispose of the land. In most African countries land tenure can only be accurately spoken of
as "communal" or tribal. Tenure can be said to be communal when the "commune" (that is, the land-holding unit)
is conceived as a social unit whose membership confers certain rights in land upon the individual and in which the individual cultivator exercises all acts of ownership except that
of alienation. Both the individual and the group enjoy certain well-defined rights in the use of land. The rural people particularly regard the land as a social unit, such as the
clan, tribe, village, and extended family. The land is the
responsibility of the head of the family, who is the caretaker.
The family is the real owner of land, but an operator can
use the land and dispose of his crop in the interest of the
community. The term community may refer to a family, a
clan, kindred or lineage group. In most of rural Africa
the land belongs to many--the living, the dead, and countless
numbers unborn. Land is an heirloom of the family, the
kinship, and the extended family. The sanction of customary
tenure against the sale or misuse of land arises from the
universal belief that the land is a sacred trust held by the
present generation of users on behalf of the dead ancestors
of the group as well as unborn generations.

"Individuals are prohibited from disposing of land of
the group either by sale or mortgage. Land is not a nego-
tiable property, and is as such not heritable and alienable
by individuals."[7] In Africa the condition of land tenure is
practically the same except for a few small differences from
country to country. With all these arrangements women are
completely excluded from tenure arrangements. The use of
land was transferable and inherited, but the evidence was
overwhelming that this power remains with the male, while
the female who mainly operates the land continues to be a
tenant.

African land arrangements are the continuity of different customary laws inherited by traditions. If the present
economies of these countries continue to pursue this develop-
mental pattern, the position of women will remain substantially unchanged. Males register the land in their names to

the disadvantage of the females who use the land for food
production. In consideration of rural development and women the women's organizations everywhere are questioning
the roles that have been assigned to them and the values on
which the roles are based. Land ownership by traditional
arrangement has not been favorable to African women, but
the women through their organizations are drawing strength
to face the challenge. The customs have assigned the males
to inherit the land in African societies, but could this sub-
jugation code of tradition be tempered so that women could
share the land rights, the women asked? All over the globe
women are coming out to speak for themselves. They boldly
speak in two camps: namely the traditional women and the
liberated women. African women surely fall into the first
camp, as they are dislocated by their economic situations.
"Though it is perhaps not always recognized, it is certainly
true that any change which would produce better conditions
for women would, in the final analysis, be most effective if
the women themselves showed awareness and expressed a
positive desire for such change."[8]

The development of agriculture is essential for the
home market and other economic activities. When the income
is derived from agriculture and the countries' activities grow
the internal market for consumer goods grows automatically,
thus enhancing the promotion of small industries. One of the
aims of rural development is to increase food production so
as to meet the needs of an expanding population. The women,
the model for peace, have openly expressed through their societies that the way to promote progress in the world is to
increase the production of food. In underdeveloped countries
agriculture and industries are complementary and not com-
petitive. In this era, if the planners and economists in Africa want to proceed with industrialization without improving the
agricultural sector of the economy, it will ruin the agricultural sector. Not to improve the lot of women in agriculture is to ruin the aim of rural development. Low productivity may be complicated, because socioeconomic structures
may contribute to the women's low standard of living. Most
of the rural women desire some sort of education, either
from their governments or United Nations organizations on
how to produce more food for the growing population.

The issue is no longer whether African women's aims
and roles are realized in the world of men, but what types
of roles are still unfulfilled? Women need programs that will
stress their important roles in rural development. Such pro-

grams will attack the symptoms of their problems and also
the basic causes that reduce the regional inequalities in per-
capita income.   We have stressed at length that women have
not been fully favored in rural development.   In this discussion we may look into some economic facts regarding rural development and women.   There are four facts that
planners, policy makers, and researchers should consider in
African rural-development plans.

1.   The demand for agricultural products is inelastic.
This is true for all cash-crop products, like palm produce,
cotton, ground nuts, and cocoa.   This means that the women
producers get less when the supply of each of these commodities is increased.   In short, it means that from most agricultural commodities, the total gross income returned to
the producers is smaller for a large crop than for smaller
crops.   This does not ensure equitable redistribution of income.

2.   The main problem of rural development is that
many women in agricultural economies are very unproductive, and as a result they have little or no income.   This
may be due to the level of technique upon the capital or upon
the nature of the crop.   In an underdeveloped economy like
that of Africa it may be right to say that with common use
of hoes and ploughs, one hundred acres of yams, coco yams,
cassava, and rice can create employment for perhaps twenty
gainfully occupied people.   Most of the women and their families are unproductive workers for many reasons: they may
lack the training or the necessary resources to enable them
to be productive as agriculturists and also may not have the
possibility of acquiring such resources.

3.   National incomes are often unequal.   During times
of rising prices those prices paid by women tend to rise more
slowly than do the prices they receive, while in the same
period the prices paid to the rural farms tend to remain fair-
ly stable.   Let us examine some of the values about the economic system which are held by the women and other rural
groups that give them political support: (a) The first value
appears to be that rural farmers have inequality of income
with the nonagricultural sector of the economy.   (b) The second value is that the nonrural people wield stronger concentrations of economic power than do the rural farms; this is
to the disadvantage of women.   The rural women cannot reduce production on the short run, while nonfarm people reduce their production in the face of declining demand.   Dur-

ing times of economic decline farmers' feelings regarding
these matters run particularly high against marketing agen-
cies--marketing board or "causa destabilization" (price assistance fund). A common sign of inequality in prices and
income can be seen in women's outcries for the improvement
of their economic and social conditions.

4. The last value held by women and rural-development planners is the one that women leaders term "women's
fundamentalism"--it is the practical difficulties that most
women have to contend with. Many men fail to gain certain
understanding of the social changes that are taking place
among women. In addition to these values regarding rural
development and women in the general economy, there is
also the one held by most researchers and scholars. They
maintain that the only way that women can embrace all the
benefits of rural development and thereby assure their position in the economy is through government intervention to
eliminate certain disparities that dishonor their status and
give advantages to the males.

REFERENCES

Chapter 1

1. A. O. Pala, African Women in Rural Development, OLC paper No. 12. Washington, D. C., 1976, p. 4.
2. E. Boserup, Women's Role in Economic Development. London: George Allen and Unwin, 1970, p. 55.
3. T. Johnson, "African Women in Their Occupations, New York Times, July 12, 1975, p. 5.
4. P. H. Gulliver, The Family Herds: A Study of Two Pastoral Tribes in East Africa. London: Routledge and Kegan Paul, 1955, p. 19.
5. Achola O. Pala, "Towards Models of Development," Signs 3, 1 (Autumn 1977), p. 9.
6. Basil Davidson, African Women's Liberation, West Africa (London), March 14, 1977, p. 497.
7. Evelyn Rich, Memo ABA Women's Riot. New York: African American Institute, 1975, p. 5.
8. Davidson, p. 497.
9. Thomas L. V. Blair, Market Survey, African Market Profile. New York: Praeger, 1965, p. 96.
10. Niara Sudarkasa, "Women and Migration in Contemporary West Africa, Signs 3, 1 (Autumn 1977), p. 182.

11.   M. E. Nzewi, "No Marriage Marker," West Africa,
       May 15, 1978, p. 936.
12.   Hariet Sibisi, "Migrants and Women Who Wait," Signs
       3,1 (Autumn 1977), p. 168.
13.   Rayna R. Reiter, Towards Anthropology of Women.
       New York: Monthly Review Press, p. 363.
14.   Joseph A. Kall, "Some Social Consistents of Indus-
       trialization," Human Organization 18, 2, (1961), p.65.
15.   Remi Cliquet, "Women's Education and Labor Force
       Participation," Signs, 3, 1(Autumn 1977), p. 250.
16.   Reiter, p. 371.
17.   Cliquet, p. 250.
18.   P. J. Foster, Africa South of the Sahara. New York:
       Macmillan, 1968, p. 116.
19.   Foster, p. 118.
20.   General Obasanjo, "Obasanjo in Kano," West Africa,
       July 3, 1978, p. 1313.

Chapter 2

1.   Charlotte Baum, Paula Hyman, and Soya Michael,
       The Jewish Woman in America. New York: Dial
       Press, 1978, p. 4.
2.   Baum, Hyman, and Michael, p. 9.
3.   Second Vatican Council, "Message to Woemn," De-
       cember 8, 1965.
4.   Tolari Awere, "Nigerian Women," Daily Times (Ni-
       geria), September 1973.
5.   Joseph Ohieku, "Women, Society, and Our Survival,"
       Catholic Secretariat (Lagos), I, 14, p. 3.
6.   Baum, Hyman, and Micahel, p. 15.
7.   Johnson, p. 3.
8.   J. F. Ade-Ajayi, Christian Mission in Nigeria, 1841-
       1897. Evanston: Northwestern University Press, p. 143.
9.   F. K. Ekechi, Missionary Enterprise and Rivalry in
       Igbo Land, 1857-1914. London: Cass, 1972, p. 25.
10.   Ibid., p. 224.
11.   Johnson, p. 5.
12.   Report by H. M. Douglas dated July 30, 1905, in
       Ekechi, p. 107.
13.   Minutes on Douglas to the Secretary (Southern Pro-
       vinces), December 28, 1918, enclosed in Moorhouse
       to Millner (confidential), January 24, 1919, in Ekechi,
       p. 213.
14.   Tugwell to Douglas, December 18, 1905, in Ekechi,
       p. 213.

15.   Ohieku, p. 3.
16.   Ekechi, p. 226.
17.   Lucy Mair, African Marriage and Social Change.
       London: Cass, 1969, p. 95.
18.   Ibid., p. 99.
19.   Titus Mbaso, "The Bantu World," in D. W. T. Shrop-
       shire, Primitive Marriage and European Law. Lon-
       don: Cass, 1970, p. 30.
20.   Baum, Hyman, and Michael, p. 7.
21.   Jane Jones, "The Women of Ohio," in Voices from
       Women's Liberation. New York: New American
       Library, 1970, p. 52.
22.   Normava Shangase, "Women in Rural Areas." Semi-
       nar on the Changing and Contemporary Role of Women
       in Society. Addis Ababa, Ethiopia, December 1-9,
       1975.

Chapter 3

1.   V. C. Uchendu, The Igbo of South East Nigeria. New
       York: Rinehart and Winston, 1965, p. 27.
2.   Ibid., p. 29.
3.   Alan Burns, The History of Nigeria. London: George
       Allen and Unwin, p. 301.
4.   Blair, p. 66.
5.   B. W. Hodder and U. I. Ukwu Markets in West Africa.
       Ibadan: Ibadan University Press, 1969, p. 175.
6.   Stewart Gillies, "Cocoa Prices Are Too High," Daily
       Express (London), October 3, 1945, p. 14.
7.   Y-Aduamah, "Madam Altastes and the Manufacturers,"
       West Africa, May 1978, p. 925.
8.   Ibid., p. 925.
9.   "Open Up the Ivory Coast," West Africa, May 1978,
       p. 1961.
10.   D. Remy, "Underdevelopment and the Experience of
       Women, Nigerian Case Study, " in Toward an Antholo-
       gy of Women. New York: Monthly Review Press,
       1975, p. 362.
11.   Baum, Hyman, and Michael, p. 125.
12.   P. Bohannan and G. Dalton, Markets in Africa. New
       York: Doubleday, 1965, p. 88.
13.   Uchendu, p. 87.
14.   B. Davidson, "African Women's Liberation," West
       Africa, March 1977, p. 497.
15.   Hodder and Ukwu, p. 175.
16.   Ibid., p. 106.

17.   Blair, p. 67.
18.   Hodder and Ukwu, p. 99.
19.   Hodder and Ukwu, p. 103.
20.   Blair, p. 67.
21.   Paul Bohannan and Philip Curtis, Africa and Africans. Garden City: Natural History Press, 1971, p. 162.
22.   Nigeria Hand Book. Lagos: Ministry of Information, 1973, p. 34.
23.   Burns, p. 207.
24.   Ekechi, p. 217.
25.   Burns, pp. 245-246.
26.   Stanley Diamond in Julian Steward, Contemporary Changes in Traditional Societies. Chicago: University of Illinois Press, 1970, p. 397.

Chapter 4

1.   G. C. Mojekwu, African Society, Culture and Politics. Washington, D.C.: University Press of America, 1977, p. 201.
2.   Ibid., p. 22
3.   Sarah Lukalo, "Role of Women in Society." Seminar on the Changing and Contemporary Role of Women in Society. Addis Ababa, Ethiopia, December 1-9, 1975.
4.   Mojekwu, p. 205.
5.   Jacob Egharabya, A Short History of Benin. Ibadan: Ibadan University Press, 1968, p. 75.
6.   S. Johnson, The History of the Yorubas from the Earliest Times to the Beginning of the British Protectorate. London: Routledge & Kegan Paul, 1969.
7.   Egharabya, p. 75.
8.   Mojekwu, p. 207.
9.   Mojekwu, p. 208.
10.   Shangase.
11.   Excerpt from papers read by delegates from Guinea-Bissau. Seminar on the Changing and Contemporary Role of Women in Society. Addis Ababa, Ethiopia, December 1-9, 1975.
12.   Robert S. McNamara (World Bank President), address on "Fertility and Development." Massachusetts Institute of Technology, 1977.

Chapter 5

1.   Sudarkasa, p. 181.

2.   Ibid., p. 182.
3.   Ibid.
4.   Ibid., p. 183.
5.   Remy, p. 361.
6.   Pala, p. 6.
7.   Bauman (1928), in Pala.
8.   A. O. Pala, "Definitions of Women and Development,"
      Signs 3, 1 (Autumn 1977), p. 12.
9.   Ibid., pp. 23-24.
10.   G. E. Currens, "Women, Men and Rice Agricultural
      Innovations in Northwestern Liberia," Human Organi-
      zation 35, 4 (Winter 1976), p. 359.
11.   Ibid., p. 359.
12.   A. O. Pala, "A Preliminary Survey of the Avenues
      for the Constraints on Women Development Process in
      Kenya." Seminar on the Changing and Contemporary
      Role of Women in Society, Addis Ababa, Ethiopia,
      December 1-9, 1975, p. 95.
13.   Ibid., p. 98.

Chapter 6

1.   John R. McClung and Thomas A. Maxwell, A Plan
      for an Agricultural Credit for Eastern Nigeria, Re-
      port No. 24, July 1967, p. 20.
2.   C. P. Lommis and J. A. Beagle, Rural Sociology.
      Englewood Cliffs: Prentice-Hall, 1957, p. 295.
3.   S. Alons, Development of Cooperatives in Eastern Ni-
      geria, Documented Report, 1961, p. 124.
4.   Pala, African Women in Rural Development, p. 13.
5.   S. N. Okpi, The Farmer's Multi-purpose Cooperative
      Society, and How to Organize One. Enugu, Nigeria:
      Ministry of Commerce, 1962, p. 29.
6.   William Bascom, The Yoruba of South Western Nigeria.
      Berkeley: University of California Press, 1969, p.
      27.
7.   Pala, African Women in Rural Development, p. 26.

Chapter 7

1.   Mohammed Harbi, Aux Originines du FLN. Paris,
      1975, p. 10.
2.   M. Yudelman, African on the Land. Cambridge:
      Harvard University Press, 1964, pp. 8-9.
3.   Pala, "Definitions of Women and Development," p. 9.
4.   B. Davidson, "African's Liberation," West Africa, March

          1977, p. 497.
5.   Boserup, pp. 55-56.
6.   May M. Edels, <u>The Chiga of Western Uganda</u>. New
          York and Oxford: University Press for International
          African Institute, 1957.
7.   Kall, p. 65.
8.   Pala, "Definitions of Women and Development," p. 34.

PROFILE OF MAJOR WOMEN'S
ORGANIZATIONS IN AFRICA

ALGERIA

A. 1) UNFA (Union Nationale des Femmes Algeriennes; National Union of Algerian Women).
  2) Address: Villa Joly 38 Ave. Franklin Roosevelt, Algiers.
B. 1) Union Panafricaine des Femmes (Pan African Union of Women).
  2) Address: 119 Didouche Mourad, Algiers.

BURUNDI

A. 1) Union des Femmes Burundaises (Union of Women of Burundi).
  2) Address: B. P. 1810, Bujumbura.
  3) Affiliations: International Democratic Federation of Women (FDIF).
  4) Principal officers appointed. Women's union is integrated into Burundi's single political party.
  5) President: Elizabeth Barak Amfiteya.
  6) Established: 1967.

7)   Activities: Promotion of women in political, economic,
      social and cultural development.

CAMEROON

A. 1) Organization des Femmes Del'Union Nationale Cam-
       erounaise (Women's Organization of the National Union
       of Cameroon).
   2) Address: B. P. 2350 Yaounde.
   3) Affiliation: Associated Country Women of the World.
   4) President: Madame Delphine Tsanga.
   5) Chapters: 42.   Individual membership 700,000.
   6) Activities: Education primary concern in rural and
       urban areas, including young women who have inter-
       rupted their schooling.   Education programs concerned
       with health and sanitation, household, and children,
       nutrition, civic and community participation, home im-
       provement, family, and national development.

CENTRAL AFRICAN REPUBLIC

A. 1) Union Des Femmes Central Africaines (UFCA) Union of
       Women of the Central African Republic.
   2) Address: B. P. 582, Bangui, Central African Repub-
       lic.
   3) Affiliation: World Movement of Mothers.
   4) President: Madame Josephine Loemba.
   5) Chapters: 25.   Individual membership 10,000.
   6) Established: 1960.
   7) Activities: Education, Literacy Courses via radio
       talks: crafts instructions etc.

DAHOMEY

A. 1) (Guides Du Dahomey) Girl Guides of Dahomey.
   2) Address: B. P. Contonu, Dahomey.
B. 1) National Council of Women of Dahomey.
   2) Address: Conseil National de la Revolution, Contonu,
       Dahomey.
   3) President: Madame Confont Adeu.

EGYPT

A. 1) Egyptian Girl Guides Association.

2)   President (by election): Prof. N. EL Ghamrawi.

3)   Individual membership 35,000.

4)   Activities: Educational, health care, family planning, service projects.

B. 1)   Egyptian Association of University Women.

2)   President Dr. Kala mawy soheir.

3)   Individual members 300

4)   Activities: Professional, social, cultural activities; participation in local Arab and international affairs.

C. 1)   National Council of Young Women's Christian Association.

2)   President (by election): Mrs. Galila Antoun.

3)   Individual membership 450.

4)   Activities: Informal Education, Illiteracy, Family planning.

D. 1)   Egyptian Women's Association.

2)   President (by election): Seyadat Maher.

3)   Individual members: 300.

4)   Established: 1943.

5)   Activities: Solving family problems, health care of children, vocational training, fighting illiteracy, aid to poor and aged, protection of mother- and child-hood.

E. 1)   Cairo Women Club.

2)   President (by election): Mrs. Aziza Hussein.

3)   Individual membership 250.

4)   Established: 1932.

5)   Activities: Rural development, family planning centre, day care centre.

F. 1)   Association in Egypt for the Protection of Women and Children.

2)   President (by election): Boussaina Aly Youssry.

3)   Individual members: 50.

4)   Established: 1912.

5)   Activities: Moral protection of women, especially unwed mothers, home for delinquent girls, prisoned women for moral offenses.

G. 1)   Hoda Charawi Association.

2)   President (by election): Mrs. Baliga Rasheed.

3)   Members 90.

4)   Established: 1923.

5)   Activities: Education, vocational training, nursing, family planning and adult education.

H. 1)   Egyptian Nursing Association.

2)   President (by election): Mrs. Kabil.

3)   Individual members 500.

4)   Established: 1951.

5)   Activities: Education professional activities, family

planning and health care.
I. 1) Egyptian Family Planning Association.
   2) President: Government Officials; Mrs. Dr. Aisha Rateb, Minister of Social Welfare.
   3) Members: About 400 Social Welfare Societies.
   4) Established: 1967.
   5) Activities: Family planning and population program of the government.

ETHIOPIA

A. 1) Young Women's Christian Association.
   2) Address: W.O. Wolete Yohannes Rd. P.O. Box 2117, Addis Ababa, Ethiopia.
   3) Affiliation: World YWCA.
   4) President: W.O. Sablewongel Yeshewalus.
   5) Chapters: Individual Members 447.
   6) Established: 1961.
   7) Activities: Literacy classes for underprivileged; Nurses aid training for dropouts, cottage industry for underprivileged girls.
B. 1) University Women Association.
   2) Address: Ethiopia National University, Addis Ababa.
   3) President: Mrs. Claire Fulass, Science Curriculum Centre.
   4) Chapters: One, Membership 50.
   5) Activities: Welfare Activities. Donations to University Students.
C. 1) Ethiopian Women's Welfare Association.
   2) Address: P.O. Box 2418, Addis Ababa, Ethiopia.
   3) Affiliation: International Alliance of Women, London: Soviet Women's Committee, Moscow.
   4) Secretary General W/o Loule Tesfaye.
   5) Established: 1934.
   6) Chapters: Branches in the 14 Provinces and 34 Centres. Individual Membership 1975-306.
   7) Activities: Education, health care, family planning and professional activities.

GABON

A. 1) UFPDG: Organization of Women of Gabon
   2) Address: B.P. 1020 Libreville, Gabon

GAMBIA

A. 1) Gambia Women's Federation.
  2) Address: B. P. Box 83, Banjul, Republic of the Gambia, West Africa.
  3) Affiliation: International Council of Women.
  4) President: Mrs. Cecilia M. R. Cole, J. P.
  5) Chapters 20: Membership about 1,000.
  6) Established: 1961.
  7) Activities: Adult literacy classes, home economics, family planning and care of babies.
B. 1) The Gambia Girl Guides Association.
  2) Address: P. O. Box 502, Banjul, Gambia.
C. 1) The Gambia Nurses Association.
  2) Address: P. O. Box 347, Benjul, Gambia.
  3) President: Mrs. Rachel Palmer.

GHANA

A. 1) Ghana Assembly of Women.
  2) Address: P. O. Box 459, Accra, Ghana.
  3) Affiliations: Associated Country Women of the World, International Alliance of Women, International Council of Women.
  4) President: Mrs. Rebecca Hutton Mills.
  5) Chapters: 21. Membership: 50.
  6) Established: 1969.
  7) Activities: Village welfare project, teaching rural women home economics and functional literacy. Coordination of women's work for the promotion of their common interests.
B. 1) Young Women's Christian Association (YWCA).
  2) Address: P. O. Box 1504, Accra, Ghana, West Africa.
  3) Affiliation: World YWCA.
  4) President: Mrs. Elsie Sowah, P. O. Box 199, Accra.
  5) Established: 1952.
  6) Chapters: 15. Memberships: 2,000.
  7) Activities: Education, health care, vocational training, rural development, leadership training.
C. 1) Christian Mothers' Association.
  2) Address: P. O. Box 5547, Accra, Ghana.
  3) Affiliation: None.
  4) President: Mrs. Monica Croffie
  5) Chapters: 150 Groups. Membership: 3,000.
  6) Established: 1962.
  7) Activities: Community development, social, religious, family planning, health care, civic education.

D. 1) Ghanaian Association of University Women.
   2) Address: Volta Hall, University of Ghana, Legon
      Ghana.
   3) Affiliation: International Federation of University Wo-
      men.
   4) President: Dr. Florence Dolphyne University of Ghana,
      Legon, Ghana.
   5) Chapters: None. Membership: 38.
   6) Established: 1968.
   7) Activities: Scholarship; Education Career Guidance
      for girls.
E. 1) Methodist Women's Fellowship Ghana.
   2) Address: P. O. Box 6290, Accra, North Ghana.
   3) Affiliation: Ghana Assembly of Women (International)
      World Federation of Methodist Women: USA, Women
      Section of Christian Council.
   4) President: Mrs. W. D. Laryea.
   5) Chapters: 5 Districts, 314 Branches. Individual Mem-
      bers over 4,000.
   6) Established: 1931.
   7) Activities: Fund raising; vocational centers; catering,
      seamstress, reading and writing, adult education cli-
      nics in rural areas.
F. 1) Women's International League for Peace and Freedom
   2) Address: P. O. Box 8365 Tenia, Ghana, W. Africa.
   3) Affiliation: International League of Peace and Free-
      dom.
   4) President: Ms. Alice Appea.
   5) Chapters: 10.
   6) Established:
   7) Activities: Adult Literacy, rural development and
      right of women.

IVORY COAST

A. 1) L'Association Des Femmes Ivoirennes (AFI).
      (Association of Women of Ivory Coast).
   2) Address: B. P. 2005, Abidjan, Ivory Coast.
   3) Affiliations: Le Conseil Internationale des Femmes
      (CIF) (in Paris). L'organization Pan-Africaine des
      Femmes (in Algiers).
   4) President: Mme. Jeanne Gervais.
   5) Chapters: 122. Population of Membership about 3
      million.
   6) Established: 1963.
   7) Activities: Education, literacy, housekeeping, family

education, civics, economic studies, political activities, household economics. AFI is tied to the government.

KENYA

A. 1) National Council of Women of Kenya.
   2) Address: P. O. Box 43741, Nairobi, Kenya.
   3) Affiliation: International Council of Women.
   4) President: Miss Mary N. Gichuru.
   5) Chapters: 20,
   6) Established: 1963.
   7) Activities: To coordinate the activities of its members, which is aimed at uplifting the status of women. Programs on education, and health.
B. 1) Maendales, ya Wanawaka (Organization for Women's Progress).
   2) Address: P. O. Box 44412.
   3) Affiliation: Associated Country Women The World: National Council of Women Kenya.
   4) President: Mrs. Jane Kians.
   5) Chapters: None. Individual members over 90,000.
   6) Established: 1950.
   7) Activities: Problems facing women in the rural areas. Adult education, child care, family living.
C. 1) Kenya Association of University Women.
   2) Address: P. O. Box 47010, Nairo, Kenya.
   3) Affiliation: International Association of University Women.
   4) Chairman: Mrs. R. Waruhui.
   5) Chapters: None. Individual members 187.
   6) Established: 1965.
   7) Activities: Education of girls, Scholarship providing meeting place for Kenyans and non-Kenyan's peers. Advancing the interests and roles of women in developing societies.
D. 1) National Nurses Association of Kenya.
   2) Address: P. O. Box 49622, Nairobi, Kenya.
   3) Affiliation: International Council of Nurses, International Confederation of Midwives, Commonwealth Nurses Federation.
   4) President: Mrs. E. M. Kiereiui.
   5) Chapters: 2. Individual members 1,400.
   6) Established: 1968.
   7) Activities: To promote nursing; to represent the interest of nursing professions: To assist members.
E. 1) International Planned Parenthood Federation, Africa Regional Office.

2) Address: P.O. Box 30234, Nairobi, Kenya.
3) Affiliation: IPPF, Central Office, London.
4) Chairman: Mr. William Wamalwa.
5) Established: 1971.
6) Chapters: 15. Individual members None.
7) Activities: Family planning, technical assistance, advisory service to family planning association in the African region education, agricultural extension etc.
F. 1) East African Women's League.
2) Address: P.O. Box 40308, Nairobi, Kenya.
G. 1) Young Women's Christian Association.
2) Address: P.O. Box 40308, Nairobi, Kenya.
H. 1) Housewives Consumer Association.
2) Address: P.O. Box 30255, Nairobi, Kenya.
I. 1) Ismaili Women's Association.
2) Address: P.O. Box 40190, Nairobi, Kenya.

LESOTHO

A. 1) Lesotho National Council of Women.
2) Address: P.O. Box 413, Maseru, Lesotho.
3) Affiliation: None.
4) President: E. Motsoane.
5) Chapters: 5. 3 Associations Membership about 2,000 each. 2 clubs membership about 200 each. Total about 6,400.
6) Established: 1967.
7) Activities: Education, small industries, domestic science subjects. Health care, home nursing, nursing. schools, adult education and community development.
B. 1) Lesotho Women's Institute.
2) Address: P.O. Box 413, Maseru, Lesotho.
3) Affiliation: None.
4) President: E.M. Mosala.
5) Established: 1961.
6) Chapters: 82 clubs. Individual membership over 2,000.
7) Activities: Handicrafts, child care, home nursing, work with nutritionists, social workers, and community development workers.
C. 1) Lesotho Home Makers Association.
2) Address: Mafeteng 218 STD Code 0506.
3) Affiliation: Associated Country Women of the World (ACWW).
4) President: Bernice T. Mohapeloa.
5) Chapters: 200. Individual Membership 3,000.

6) Established: 1935.
7) Activities: Adult Education, hygiene, nutrition, domestic science subjects and gardening.
D. 1) Boiteko Women's Association.
2) Address: P.O. Box 2046.
3) Affiliation: None.
4) President: M. Motsoane.
5) Chapters: 76 clubs. Individual membership about 1,800.
6) Established: 1961.
7) Activities: Adult Education, health care, handicrafts, and domestic science work.
E. 1) Business and Professional Women's Club of Lesotho (LBPWC).
2) Address: P.O. Box 844, Maseru, Lesotho.
3) Affiliation: None.
4) President: Mrs. Christian Sauli.
5) Chapters: 21. Membership 53.
6) Established: 1951.
7) Activities: To encourage and motivate business and professional women (BPW); to improve academic education of BPW; to work to remove sex discrimination in opportunities of employment.
F. 1) Setsoto Thota Moli.
2) Address: P.O. Mosenod, Letsoto.
3) President: Mrs. A. Nteso.
4) Goal: Self reliance.
G. 1) Roma Home Stars
2) President: Mrs. M. Makuta.
3) Goal: Cultural Advancement.

LIBERIA

A. 1) The Liberian Girl Guides Association
2) Address: 42 Carey Street, P.O. Box 706, Monrovia, Liberia.
3) Affiliation: The World Association of Girl Guides and Girl Scouts (WAGGS).
4) President: Mrs. Victoria Tolbert.
5) Chapters: 18. Membership: 985.
6) Established: 1920's.
7) Activities: Community development, service projects, youth education handicrafts, old home visits.
B. 1) Monrovia YWCA.
2) Address: P.O. Box 118, Sinkor, Liberia.
3) Affiliation: World YWCA.

4) President: Ayo Cummings
5) Established: 1941.
6) Chapters: 9. Individual membership.
7) Activities: Development, literacy, health and nutrition, program planning.
C. 1) Federation of Liberian Women
2) Address: P. O. Box 1002, Monrovia, Liberia.
3) President: Ms. Nancy Ross.
D. 1) Zonta International Club.
2) Address: P. O. Box 1002, Monrovia, Liberia.
3) President: Ms. Edith Bright.
E. 1) Liberian Nurses Association.
2) Address: John F. Kennedy National Medical Centre,
   Monrovia, Liberia.
3) President: Ms. Mable Yaidoo.

LIBYAN ARAB REPUBLIC

A. 1) Sh Taniq No 4.
   Tripoli, Libyan Arab Republic.
2) President: Mrs. Khadija Al Jahmi.

MALAGASY REPUBLIC

A. 1) Conseil National Des Associations De Femmes De
   Madagascar (National Council of Women's Associations
   of Madagascar).
2) Address: 90 bis Lalana Lt. Andrian aronanana, Tana-
   rive, Madagascar.
3) Affiliation: International Council of Women, Pan African Organization of Women
4) President: Mme. Ramarosaona Zaiveline, 90 bis
   avenue, Marechal Foch, Tananarive.
5) Established: 1967.
6) Chapters: 12. Membership: 50.
7) Activities: Citizen education.
B. 1) Dorcas
2) Address: Lot UB81, Antashabe Ambatoroka routed,
   Ambohipo, Tananarive, Malagasy.
3) President: Mme. Ramantsiahna.
4) Established: 1969.
5) Chapters: 2, 500 churches have groups. Individual
   members 12, 500.
6) Activities: Training of women, child care and hygiene;
   rural development.

C. 1) Women's Department of Protestant Church in Madagascar.
   2) Address: 50, Road George V., Faravolictra, Tananarive, Malagasy Republic.
   3) Affiliation: COE.
   4) President: Mme. Louise Rosendra hasina, Lot UB8IC, Antashabe Ambatoroka Lalana Ambohipo, Tananarive.
   5) Chapters: Two churches. Affiliated: Individual members.
   6) Established: 1974.
   7) Activities: Help girl develop intellectually and spiritually, reading, writing and handicrafts.

D. 1) Fianakaviana Sambatra (Family Planning Organization of Malagasy).
   2) Affiliation: International Planned Parenthood Federation (IPPF).
   3) President: Mrs. Alice Rajaonah.
   4) Chapters: Individual members 10,098.
   5) Established: 1967.
   6) Activities: Family welfare, sex education, nutrition and health.

E. 1) Fikambanana Kristiana Ho An'ny Zatovo Vavy Eto Madagasikara (Young Women's Christian Associations of Madagasikara).
   2) Address: Lot IVD-18A Behorirka Antananarivo/Madagasikara B. P. 1140.
   3) Affiliation: World YWCA.

F. 1) National Union of Catholic Women's Organizations In Madagascar.
   2) Address: 102 bis, Lalana Lenine, Tananarive, Madagascar.

G. 1) Protestant Women's Association.
   2) Address: B. P. 1184, Fianarantosoa, Madagascar.

H. 1) National Committee for the Protection of Women.
   2) Address: Lot 11K-6 Andravoahangy Tananarive, Madagascar.

I. 1) Women's Physician's Association
   2) Address: Lot IV093 bis Isotry Tananarive, Madagascar.

MALAWI

A. 1) League of Malawi Women.
   2) Address: Malawi Congress Party National Headquarters, Box 5250, Limbe, Malawi.

MALI

A. 1) Union Nationale Des Femmes Du Mali (UNFM). (National Union of Women of Mali).
   2) Address: National Directorate of Social Affairs, Bamko, Mali.
   3) Affiliation: Pan African Organization of Women, Algiers (OPF).
   4) President: Mme. Traere Mariame.
   5) Chapters: Individual members.
   6) Established: 1968.
   7) Activities: To raise the consciousness of women as citizens; defend women's interest within the family. Fight Emancipation and development of Women.

MAURITANIA

A. 1) Mouvement Nationale Des Femmes Du Parti Du Peuple Mauritanieu (National Women's Movement of the People's Party of Mauritania).
   2) Address: Conseil Superieur des Femmes B. P. 47 Nouakclott, Mauritania.
   3) Affiliations: OPF, Pan African Women's Organization; UMOF.
B. 1) Magheb International Union of Family Groups; International Federation of Family Lawyers and Social Workers.
   2) President: Toure Aissata Kane.
   3) Chapter: Individual members 253,144.
   4) Established: 1961.
   5) Activities: Education; Information health, status of women, economic development, cooperative works, cultural development.

MAURITIUS

A. 1) Mauritius Girl Guides Association.
   2) Address: Acting Island Commissioner Flat Caltex, Kennedy Avenue, Vacoas, Mauritius.
   3) Affiliation: World Association of Guides.
   4) President: Ms. Irene Colin.
   5) Chapters: None. Individual members 797.
   6) Established: 1926.
   7) Activities: Development, social service, cultural and traditional crafts.

B. 1)   Women's Self-Help Association.
   2)   Address: Concordite Club, Lees Street, Curepipe,
        Mauritius.
   3)   Affiliation: International Alliance of Women.
   4)   President: Mrs. K. Currimjee.
   5)   Chapters: Individual members.
   6)   Established: 1969.
   7)   Activities: Marketing, dressmaking, promotion of
        social progress among women in the rural areas.
C. 1)   Les Ecoles Ménageres (Schools for Home Economics).
   2)   Address: 42 Rue Pope Hennessy, Port Louis, Mauri-
        tius.
   3)   Affiliation: World Union of Catholic Women Organi-
        zations (WUCWO).
   4)   President: Ms. France Boyer de La Gireday.
   5)   Chapters: 40 centres.   Individual members.
   6)   Established: 1956.
   7)   Activities: House economics, women education and
        civics.
D. 1)   Action Familiale (Family Planning).
   2)   Address: Royal Road, Rose Hill, Mauritius.
   3)   Affiliation: International Federation for Family Life
        promotion.
   4)   President: Dr. Pierre Piat.
   5)   Chapters: Individual members 10,950.
   6)   Established: 1963.
   7)   Activities: Family planning; counselling, birth control
        campaign, maternity and child care.
E. 1)   Women's Associations, Mauritius.
   2)   Address: Social welfare division; Ministry of Social
        Security, 13-21 Edith Cavell St. , Port Louis, Mauritius.
   3)   President: Mrs. G. Mootosamy, M.B.E.

MOROCCO

A. 1)   Association Maricaine De Plantification Familiale.
   2)   Address: 6 Rue 16N E1 Kadi Quartier, Des Orangers,
        P.O. Box 1217, Rabat R.P., Morocco.
   3)   Affiliation: International Planned Parenthood Federa-
        tion (IPPF).
   4)   President: Mme. Zahra Doukkali.
   5)   Chapters: 4; Individual members 88.
   6)   Established: 1971.
   7)   Activities: Information, education and family planning.
B. 1)   Union Nationale Des Femmes Marocaines.
   2)   Address: 3, Rue El Afghani Victor Hugo, P.O. Box
        30, Rabat, Morocco.

3) Affiliation: Arab League of Organizations of African Women.
4) President: Princess Lalla Fatima Zohra.
5) Chapters: 25 provincial Committees.   Individual members.
6) Established: 1969.
7) Activities: Women's education, family planning and women development.

NIGER

A. 1) Contact: Mlle. Gany Djaroumeye Coordinator for International Women's Year.
2) Address: Ministry of Foreign Affairs Niamey, Niger.

NIGERIA

A. 1) National Council of Women's Societies, Nigeria.
2) Address: I. Tafawa Balewa Square, Lagos, Federal Republic of Nigeria.
3) Affiliations: ICW, IAW, Pan African Women's Organization ACWW.
4) President: Chief Mrs. K. A. Pratt.
5) Chapters: 419.   Individual Membership 164.
6) Established: 1958.
7) Activities: Education, Nigerian Women's Day, economics and promotion of women's activities, nursery centres and scholarships.
B. 1) Lagos State Market Women's Association.
2) Address: Iyun Road, Surulere, Lagos, Nigeria.
3) Affiliation: National Council of Women's Societies, Nigeria.
4) President: Mrs. M. Caxton-Marins.
5) Chapters: 5.   Individual members 3,000.
6) Established: 1965.
7) Activities: Progress of the Country: Marketing and rural development.
C. 1) The Nigerian Girl Guides Association.
2) Address: 25 Obalende Rd.   P. O. Box 640, Lagos, Nigeria.
3) Affiliation: Member of the World Association of Girl Guides and Girl Scouts.
4) President: Vacant.
Vice President: Vacant.
5) Chapters: Individual members.

6)   Established: 1919.
7)   Activities: Development of characters; arts & cultures, vocational centres, fund raising.
D. 1)   University of Lagos Women Society.
2)   Address: University of Lagos Campus Yaba, Lagos, Nigeria.
3)   Affiliation: National Council of Women's Societies, Lagos.
4)   President: Mrs. Christie Ade Ajayi.
5)   Chapters: None.   Individual members 500.
6)   Established: 1965.
7)   Activities: Nursery School; fund raising, visits to handicapped children.
E. 1)   International Women's Society, Lagos.
2)   Address: P.O. Box 2304, Lagos, Nigeria.
3)   Affiliation: National Council of Women of Nigeria.
4)   President: Mrs. Elizabeth Paul.
5)   Chapters: None.   Individual members 250.
6)   Established:
7)   Activities: Nursery, Library Services, aids to women beggars, teaching the blind, home visits to the elderly, education and home management training.
F. 1)   Nigerian Women's Party.
2)   Address: 45 Falolu St, Surulere Lagos, Nigeria.
3)   President: Mrs. T. Dedeke.
G. 1)   Young Women's Christian Association.
2)   Address: Moloney St. Lagos, Nigeria.
3)   President: Lady Ayo Alakija.
H. 1)   Professional Women's Association.
2)   Address: Dental Centre Lagos, Nigeria.
3)   President: Dr. Simi Johnson.
I. 1)   Nigerian Association of Women Lawyers.
2)   Address: c/o Mrs. M.O. Akintola 13, Catholic Mission, St. P.O. 633 Lagos, Nigeria.

RWANDA

A. 1)   Association Femme D'Assistance AUX Femmes Et Enfant Rwandais (Women's organization to assist women and children of Rwanda).
2)   Address: B.P. 747 Kigali, Rwanda.
3)   Affiliation: None.
4)   President: A. Cyimana.
5)   Chapters: 3 Individual members.
6)   Established: 1965.
7)   Activities: Development of women and children, community development projects.

B.1) "A prefer" Association pour la Promotion de la
      Femme Rwandaise (Association for the Advancement
      of the Women of Rwanda).
  2) Address: B.P. 496 Kigali, Rwanda.
  3) Affiliation: None.
  4) President: Mrs. Scolastique Naaruhutse.
  5) Chapters: Individual members 100.
  6) Established: 1967.
  7) Activities: Development.
C.1) L'Association pour la Promotion de la Femme.
      (Association for the advancement of women).
  2) Address: B.P. 60 Kigali, Rwanda.

SENEGAL

A.1) Association Pour L'Action Sociale Des Femmes De
      Rufisque (AAS) Association for Social Action by the
      Women Rufisque.
  2) Address: Boulevard Maurice Queye Rufisque, Senegal.
  3) Affiliation: International Sonoptimist Club of Dakar.
  4) President: Madam N'Deye Coumba M'Benguie.
  5) Chapters: None. Individual members 645.
  6) Established: 1969.
  7) Activities: Family planning, education and training
      programs, domestic science training; and government
      programs.
B.1) Zonta Club of Dakar.
  2) Address: P.O. Box 1724, Dakar, Senegal.
  3) Affiliation: Zonta International, Chicago, USA.
  4) President: Janine N'Diaye.
  5) Chapters: None. Members 46.
  6) Established: 1969.
  7) Activities: Health care, struggle against poliomyelitis.
C.1) Union Nationale Des Femmes Da Senegal (National
      Union of Women of Senegal) Assemblee National, Da-
      kar, Senegal.
  2) President: Mme. Caroline Diop.
D.1) Les Femmes De La Promotion Humaine (Women for
      Human Development).
  2) Address: Secretariat d'Etat ala Promotion Humaine
      Building, Adminitratif, Dakar, Senegal. Attention:
      Mlle Khady Queye.

SIERRA LEONE

A.1) National Federation of Sierra Leone Women's Or-

ganization.
2) Address: P.O. Box 811, Freetown, Sierra Leone.
3) Affiliation: International Council of Women, Paris, France.
4) President: Miranda P.A. Coker.
5) Chapters: 42 female groups. Individual memberships 10.
6) Established: 1959.
7) Activities: Eradication of illiteracy, and out of school education. Unity of women, rights and privileges of women. Sponsored a school at Shenga.
B.1) Sierra Leone Muslim Women's Association Kankaylay.
2) Address: P.O. Box 1168, Freetown, Sierra Leone.
3) Affiliation: None.
4) President: Haja Saramba Korama.
5) Chapters: 10. Individual members 7,500.
6) Established: 1972.
7) Activities: Literacy class for adults and children, scholarship awards, institution for girls.
C.1) Young Women's Christian Association of Sierra Leone (YWCA).
2) Address: P.O. Box 511, Bismark Johnson Street, Brookfield, Freetown, Sierra Leone.
3) Affiliation: World YWCA.
4) President: Mrs. Naomi Odesimi-John.
5) Chapters: None. Individual members 5,000.
6) Established: 1915.
7) Activities: Literacy classes, educational project; nursery schools.
D.1) Sierra Leone Girl Guides Association.
2) Address: P.O. Box 954, I George St. Freetown, Sierra Leone.
3) Affiliation: World Association of Girl Guides and Girl Scouts.
4) President: Lady M. Bankole-Jones.
5) Chapters: None. Individual members 3,200.
6) Established: 1924.
7) Activities: Homemaking; individual help; development of individuals and sports.
E.1) Sierra Leone Muslim Women's Benevolent Organization.
2) Address: 29 Messirni Street, Makeni, Sierra Leone.
3) Affiliation: None.
4) President: Mrs. Hawa Kanu.
5) Established: 1971.
6) Chapters: None. Individual members 300.
7) Activities: Award of scholarships, orphanage care, counselling, literacy classes and charities.
F.1) Sierra Leone Nurses Association.

2) Address: Post Office Box 971, Freetown, Sierra Leone.
3) Affiliations: International Council of Nurses; Commonwealth Nurses Federation.
4) President: Mrs. J. M. Palmer.
5) Chapters: None. Individual members 140.
6) Established: 1961.
7) Activities: Development of nursing education and professional nursing standard and ethical conduct. To improve economic conditions of the nurses.

G. 1) Sierra Leone Midwives Association.
2) Address: P. O. Box 1394, Freetown, Sierra Leone.
3) Affiliation: Member of International Confederation of Midwives.
4) President: Mrs. M. A. Fraser.
5) Chapters: None. Individual members 115.
6) Established: 1969.
7) Activities: Health education and nutrition, family plannign, maternity and child health care.

H. 1) Planned Parenthood Association.
2) Address: P. O. Box 1094, Freetown, Sierra Leone.
3) Affiliation: International Planned Parenthood Federation (IPPF).
4) President: Dr. June Holst Rones
5) Chapters: None. Individual members 160.
6) Established: 1958.
7) Activities: Family planning, maternity and child health care, cancer research; education and training, infertility studies.

SOMALIA

A. 1) Women's Section, Political Affairs Department, Presidency of the Supreme Revolutionary Council.
2) Address: Mogadishu, Somali Democratic Republic, East Africa.

SOUTH AFRICA

A. 1) National Council of Women of South Africa (NCW).
2) Address: 207/8 Standard Bank ABC Chambers, 153 Main Street, Port Elizabeth 6001, South Africa.
3) Affiliation: The International Council of Women.
4) President: Mrs. J. S. Mann.
5) Chapters: 30; 543 Affiliated Societies. Individual members 1641.

6) Established: 1911.
7) Activities: Arts, home economics, relation and peace, migration, media women and employment. Recommendations are made to government.
B. 1) Young Women's Christian Association of South Africa (YWCA).
2) Address: P. O. Box 31580, Braam fontein Johannesburg 2017, South Africa.
3) Affiliation: Affiliated to World YWCA Geneva.
4) President: Ms. Jane Phakathi.
5) Chapters: 8. Individual members about 4,000.
6) Established: 1948.
7) Activities: Informal education, health and nutrition, family planning, literacy, home industries, youth leadership training for young adults, Legal Disabilities of South African Women.
C. 1) The Black Sash.
2) Address: 501, Lester House, 58 Marshall Street, Johannesburg 2001, South Africa.
3) President: Mrs. Joyce Harris.
4) Affiliation: None.
5) Chapters: 7. Individual members 1,100.
6) Established: 1955.
7) Activities: Pressure group, position of legislation, events and trends, assists African people in their difficulties, plight of African women. Just society for all societies.
D. 1) South Africa Federation of Business and Professional Women's Clubs.
2) Address: P.O. Box 347, Somerset West 7130, R. South Africa.
3) Affiliation: International Federation of Business and Professional Women.
4) President: Mrs. Zerilda Droskie.
5) Chapters: 20. Individual Members about 1,000.
6) Established: 1949.
7) To ensure continuation of high standard. To achieve equal status for women in economic, civil and political life.
E. 1) South Africa Association of University Women.
2) Address: 501 L'Hiroudelle, 157 Relly St. Sunnyside, Pretoria 0002, South Africa.
3) Affiliation: International Federation of University Women.
4) President: Miss Joan S. Whitmore.
5) Chapters: 12. Individual members about 850.
6) Established: 1922.

7) Activities: High education for women, to improve opportunity for employment. Improvement of legal, fis-
cal and economic status of women. Welfare related
to children and women. Scholarship awards to non-
white women in the University.

F. 1) Women in Action.
2) Address: 63 Vause Road, Durban 4001 South Africa.
3) Affiliation: South African National Council of Women
4) Principal Officer: Volunteers.
5) Chapters: None. Individual members 90.
6) Established: 1973.
7) Activities: Promotion equality of women, local issues
are pursued on an ad hoc basis, consciousness on the
status of women in South Africa.

G. 1) Abortion Reform Action Group.
2) Address: 9 Woodside Avenue, Cowies Hill 3600, Natal, South Africa.
3) Affiliation: Abortion Law Reform Association, United
Kingdom.
4) President: Ms. June Cope.
5) Chapters: One branch, Liaison officers. Individual
members 167.
6) Established: 1972.
7) Activities: Reform of abortion and sterilization law
to incorporate early abortion procedure into existing
family planning services.

H. 1) South African Medical Women's Association, Natal.
2) Address: Secretary, 2 Woodlands Avenue, Westville
3630, Natal, South Africa.
3) Affiliation: Medical Women International Association.
4) President: Prof. J. N. Scragg.
5) Chapters: None. Individual members 42.
6) Established: 1958.
7) Activities: Family planning, nutrition services.

I. 1) Women's Federation.
2) Address: P. O. Box 79 Clernaville 3602 Natal (RSA)
South Africa.
3) Affiliation: None.
4) President: Fatimer Meer.
5) Chapters: 20; Individual members 2,000.
6) Established: 1973.
7) Activities: Cultural, educational, professional: encouraging women in home, industries and business
methods. Development of black community by black
women.

SUDAN

A. 1) National Commission on the Status of Women.
   2) Address: Ministry of youth and sports, social welfare, Khartoum, Sudan.
   3) Chairman: Dr. Fatima Abdel Mahmoud.
   4) Chapters: None. 20 members of Government Ministries.
   5) Activities: Women's Affairs mainly.
B. 1) Sudanese Women Union.
   2) Established: 1971.
   3) Chapters: None. Membership 3/4 million.
   4) Activities: Popular women's movement and women's voluntary organizations
C. 1) Women's Secretariat.
   2) Activities: Political organization, development plans and programs.

SWAZILAND

A. 1) Zondle Women's Organization.
   2) Address: P. O. Box 472 Mbabane, Swaziland.
   3) Affiliation: (Swaziland Branch).
   4) President: Mrs. Evelyn Sukati.
   5) Chapters: 4. Individual members 560.
   6) Established: 1968.
   7) Activities: Household management, hygiene, family planning, infant care and nutrition.
B. 1) The Swaziland Young Women's Christian Association.
   2) Address: P. O. Box 39, Mbabane, Swaziland.
   3) Affiliation: Swaziland YWCA was introduced to the world YWCA seeking affiliation.
   4) President: Mrs. Sithebe.
   5) Chapters: Individual members 300.
   6) Established: 1958.
   7) Activities: Education, literacy classes, nutrition, child welfare, family planning.
C. 1) Lutsango Women's Organization.
   2) Address: P. O. Box 338, Mbabane Swaziland.
   3) President: Mrs. R. Mdladla.

TANZANIA

A. 1) Umoja Wa Wanawaka Wa Tanganyika (United Women of Tanzania).

2) Address: P. O. Box 1473, Dar Salaam Tanzania.
3) Affiliation: None.
4) Chairman: Mrs. Sofia Kawawa.
5) Chapters: Individual members about 1 million.
6) Established: 1962.
7) Activities: Joining all women together development
    of economics, political and social of the nation and the
    world. To cooperate and work with the Government
    and party on all matters of special concern to women.
    Preserve the rights and destiny of women in our na-
    tion, in the rest of Africa and the world.
B. 1) Tanzania Girl Guides Association.
2) Address: P. O. Box 424, Dar Es Salaam Tanzania.
3) Affiliation: All national organizations of girl scouts
    and girl guides.
4) Chairman: Mrs. Martha C. Bulengo.
5) Chapters: Individual members 7, 048.
6) Established: 1928.
7) Activities: Camp activities, cottage industries taught,
    development projects.   Promote a full sense of citizen-
    ship by training habits of observation, obedience, con-
    fidence and self-reliance.

TUNISIA

A. 1) Union Nationale Des Femmes De Tunisie.
2) Address: 56 Boulevard Bab Benat, Tunis, Tunisia.
3) Affiliation: CIF.
4) President: Fathia Mzali.
5) Chapters: 280.   Individual members 37, 000.
6) Established: 1956.
7) Activities: Education, family planning, child care
    centres, development.
B. 1) Tunisia Family Planning Association.
2) Address: 80 Avenue Hedi Chaker, Tunis, Tunisia.
3) Affiliation: IPPF.
4) President: Dr. Ottman Sfar.
5) Established: 1969.
6) Chapters: Individual membership 30, 000 to 35, 000.
7) Activities: Family planning.

UGANDA

A. 1) Young Women's Christian Association of Uganda (YWCA).
2) Address: P. O. Box 2108, Kampala, Uganda.

3) Affiliation: World YWCA, Geneva, Switzerland, National Council of social welfare.
4) President: Mrs. Mary Kasozi-Kaya.
5) Established: 1952.
6) Chapters: about 200 clubs. Individual members 6,000.
7) Activities: Educational programs, rural development, literacy training, projects in agriculture, nutrition and model farm.
B.1) Women's Organization of Uganda.
2) Address: P.O. Box 7136, Kampala Uganda.
3) Chairman: Ms. Anna Bagenda.
C.1) Uganda Girl Guides Association.
2) Address: P.O. Box 696, Kampala, Uganda.

UPPER VOLTA

A.1) Federation Des Femmes Votaiques (FFV).
2) Address: B.P. 378 Ouagadougou, Upper Volta.
3) Affiliation: Alliance Internationale des Femmes.
4) President: Jeanne Zongo.
5) Chapters: Individual members 1,500.
6) Established: 1974.
7) Activities: child care centres, education, literacy and family planning.

ZAIRE

A.1) Association of Baptist Women in CBZ.
2) Address: B.P. 4728 Kinshasa II, Zaire.
3) Affiliation: Baptist World Alliance.
4) President: Lala K. Biasima.
5) Chapters: 500. Individual members 3,000.
6) Established: 1958.
7) Activities: Christian education, evangelization education, literacy, family planning.
B.1) Federation des Guides (Federation of Girl Guides).
2) Address: B.P. 3014, Kalina, Kinshasa, Zaire.
C.1) Les Femmes des CBZO (Women of CBZO).
2) Address: B.P. 4728 Kinshasa, Zaire.
3) President: Choyenne Lala.

ZAMBIA

A.1) The Young Women's Christian Association Council of

Zambia (YWCA).
2) Address: P.O. Box RW 115, Lusaka, Zambia.
3) Affiliation: World YWCA.
4) President: Miss Jean Mwondela.
5) Chapters: Individual members.
6) Established: 1957.
7) Activities: Education of women and girls; vocational programs: affiliated with women brigade which is part of political governing body of the country.
B.1) National Association of Business and Professional Women of Zambia.
2) Address: P.O. Box 333, Lusaka, Zambia.
3) Affiliation: International Federation of Business and Professional Women.
4) Chapter: 5 clubs. Individual members 200.
5) Established: 1964.
6) Activities: Education and training of Zambian girls, liaison with appropriate Government Ministers.
C.1) Zambia Nurses Association.
2) Address: P.O. Box 2104, Kitwe, Zambia.
3) Affiliation: International Council of Nurses, Commonwealth Nurses Association.
4) Chapters: 8 branches; 8 provinces; Individual members 230.
5) Established: 1950.
6) President: Mrs. Eva Saunderson.
7) Activities: Fostering unity among nurses. To raise the status of women, maintain the integrity and to promote the integrity of the nurses.
D.1) Girl Guides Association.
2) Address: Argyll Road, Lusaka Zambia.
E.1) Lusaka Women's Institute.
2) Address: P.O. Box 1333, Lusaka, Zamiba.
F. 1) Women Brigade.
2) Address: c/o UNIP, P.O. Box 302, Lusaka, Zambia.

ZIMBABWE

A.1) Young Women's Christian Association (YWCA).
2) Address: P.O. Box 3170 Salisbury Bible house 99 Victoria Street, Salisbury, Rhodesia.
3) Affiliation: World Affiliated to the World YWCA with headquarters in Geneva.
4) President: Mrs. Agnes Dhlula.
5) Chapters: 64. Individual members 1,000.
6) Established: 1957.

7) Activities: Education, youth, leadership, health, rural development youth work.
B.1) National Federation of Business and Professional Women of Rhodesia.
2) Address: 140 Main Street, Umtali Rhodesia.
3) Affiliation: International Federation of Business and Professional Women.
4) President: Mrs. Jonah Woods.
5) Chapters: 6. Individual members 300.
6) Established: 1949.
7) Activities: Promote Professional and Business Women; Education employment conditions; health, legislation U. N. ESCO and status of women.
C.1) Rhodesian Association of University Women.
2) Address: P. O. Box 8223 Causeway, Salisbury, Rhodesia.
3) Affiliation: International Federation of University Women.
4) President: Mrs. Helen Hyslop.
5) Chapters: Individual members 150.
6) Established: 1956.
7) Activities: Education and status of women; scholarship award to African girls; cultural meeting.
D.1) Rhodesia Nurses Associations.
2) Address: P. O. Box 1202, Bulawayo, Rhodesia.
3) Affiliation: Members of International Nursing Council.

PAN-AFRICAN RESEARCH CENTRE FOR WOMEN (UNITED NATIONS) (By the courtesy of Mrs. Arvonne Fraser, Coordinator Women in Development A. I. D. Washington, D. C. 20523)

2) Address: Economic Commission for Africa ECA, P. O. Box 3001, Addis Ababa, Ethiopia.
3) Affiliation: Is part of the United Nations.
4) President: Excutive Secretary of the Economics Commission for Africa is over all head.
5) Consultant: Margret Snyder.
6) Chapters: The Centre serves all women of Africa (State members of ECA).
7) Established: 1975: will assume and intensify activities of the ECA women's program which was established in 1971.
8) Language: English, French and Arabic to be used.
9) Activities and Functions
Main activities are on training, research, and infor-

mation on subjects such as food, and nutrition, including food production, nutritional policy and programs,
food distribution storage and preservation, handicrafts
and small scale business and industries, management
of family resources, budgeting, use of labour-saving
devices and home improvement, project planning, up-
grading of wage-employed women; integration of women in national areas.

10) Achievements: Centre's activities--one aimed at improving the position of women in national development
programs in African countries.

TABLES

Table 1

Women and Farm Activities

Female University Enrollment in Cameroun and the Ivory
Coast by Type of Studies (% of all students)

	Cameroun	France	Ivory Coast
Faculty of Law	4	29	3
Faculty of Social Science & Fine Arts	14	63	20
Faculty of Sciences	7	32	6
Faculty of Medicine & Pharmacy	12	33	7
Ecole Normale Superieure	14	n. a.	6
Total	8	42	8

Source: For France 1961-62 data from P. Bourdieu and
J. C. Passeron, Paris, Edition de Minuit, 1970;
for Cameroun, Statistics du Ministiere, 1970-71;
for Ivory Coast, UNESCO, 1974. Vide Remi Cliquet, Signs, 3, (1977), p. 254.

Table 2

University of Nigeria's
Enrollment Statistics

| | 1964 | | 1965 | |
Faculty	Male	Female	Male	Female
Agriculture	218	22	323	28
Arts	244	45	294	46
Business	257	13	363	19
Education	239	21	349	32
Law	56	7	80	10
Engineering	174	-	222	-
Science	215	26	288	39
Social Studies	287	5	372	14
Total	1,690	139	2,291	188

Source: Statistical Digest, 1966; Eastern Nigeria, Enugu,
        p. 341.

Table 3

Women and Farm Activities

Month	Farm Activity	Total Days
January	Repair of the fences, storage, cleaning and bagging of grains	25 man-days 17 woman-days
February	Road repairs, plough repairs, bagging, storage and final threshing, etc.	25 man-days 2 woman-days
March	Preliminary clearing, general maintenance, general work at house, marketing	26 man-days 4 woman-days
April	Plough and ridge for millet, guinea corn, general work, etc.	26-1/2 man-days 3 woman-days
May	Finish guinea corn cultivation, sowing ground nuts, weeding, sowing vegetables in the garden, general work	35 man-days 10 woman-days
June	Guinea corn 2nd weeding and threshing, commerce, plough and ridge for cotton, complete ploughing, manuring for ground nuts, sow beans, sow tobacco, general work	46 man-days 39 woman-days
July	3rd weeding, moulding of guinea corn, harvesting millet, plant tobacco, sweet potatoes	40 man-days 20 woman-days
August	Complete harvesting of millet, 4th weeding of guinea corn if necessary, moulding of ground nuts continues, weeding of garden crops	24 man-days 22 woman-days
September	Check baskets and bags for harvest of ground nuts, maintenance, drainage and solid conservation, cut pastures	24-1/2 man-days 8 woman-days

October	Prepare site for stack of millet, guinea corn, harvest ground nuts, picking and drying of ground nuts, cutting over pastures	29 man-days 30 woman-days
November	Harvest guinea corn, millet, lay in furrows, remove heads and stack, harvest first cotton, picking and drying of ground nuts, shelling, etc., miscellaneous harvesting	40 man-days 78 woman-days
December	Threshing of guinea corn, collecting stalks, 2nd and 3rd harvesting of cotton and marketing, shelling, bagging and marketing of ground nuts	28 man-days 30 woman-days

Source: T. A. Phillips, <u>Farm Management in West Africa</u>. London: Longmans, Green and Co., 1961, pp. 70-72.

Table 4

Available Labor from a Settler's Family

A married couple with six children:

Man = 300 man-days per annum
Wife = 200 man-days per annum
Children (2 grown) = 100 man-days per annum
Total = 600 man-days per annum

Source: Eastern Nigerian Farm Settlement Scheme,
Technical Bulletin No. 6, p. 61.

Estimated Annual Labor Requirement of the Holding
in the Different Types of Farm Settlement

15 Acres Oil Palm/Rubber Holding

Acreage	Crop	Man-days/AC/Annum	Total
4.0	Rubber	83	332
8.0	Oil Palm	26	208
2.5	Arable	334	167
0.5	Homestead	-	190
		Total	897

Labor deficit = 897 - 600
            = 297 man-days per annum

16 Acres Oil Palm/Cacao Holding

Acreage	Crop	Man-days/AC/Annum	Total
5.0	Oil Palm	26	130
8.0	Cacao	30	240
2.5	Arable	334	167
0.5	Homestead	11	190
		Total	727

Labor deficit = 727 - 600
            = 127 man-days per annum

16 Acres Oil Palm/Citrus Holding

Acreage	Crop	Man-days/AC/Annum	Total
9.0	Oil Palm	26	234
4.0	Citrus	36	144
2.5	Arable	334	165
0.5	Homestead	-	190
		Total	735

Labor deficit = 735 - 600
= 135 man-days per annum

1. The calculation is based on a working day of eight hours. When the settlers become self-employed, a working day will be considerably longer than eight hours since evening work would be undertaken.
2. The total additional labor required in a settlement is given below:

Annual Labor Deficit Number of Settlers

Example: Oil Palm/Rubber Settlement =

$$\frac{297 \times 720}{300} = 712.8 \text{ man-days}$$

Source: Eastern Nigerian Farm Settlement Scheme, Technical Bulletin No. 6, p. 61

Table 5

Implements and Women

Implement	£	S	D
Farmer A			
1 large hoe (galma) for self			
(lasts 3 years)	-	6	-
1 large hoe for boys aged thirteen	-	5	-
2 small hoes (obtained in return			
for 2 old hoes)	-	-	-
2 more small hoes at 1s :3d each	-	2	6
1 magirbi (harvesting tool)	-	1	-
2 axes	-	2	6
Total cash outlay on farm im-			
plements	-	17	0
Farmer B			
1 large hoe (second hand)	-	2	6
1 small hoe	-	-	9
1 knife	-	-	2
1 lanje (grass cutter)	-	-	2
Total cash outlay on im-			
plements	-	3	7

Source: H. A. Oluwashanmi, Agriculture and Nigerian Economic Development.   Oxford University Press, 1966,
p. 83.

Table 6

Personal Rice Fields

No. of Persons in Household	No. of Fields	Household Members With Personal Fields
4	1	2 wives together (1)
8	1	mother (1)
8	2	sons (2)
8	4	wives (4)
9	2	sons (2)
12	5	wives (2), daughters (2), son's wife (1)

No. of Persons in Household	No. of Fields	Household Members With Personal Fields
14	2	sons (2)
14	3	wives (3)
15	5	wives (5)
18	4	wives (3), mother (1)
24	6	sons (5), helper (1)
27	1	younger brother, nephew together (1)
27	4	wives (2), mother (1), younger brother (1)

Note: Total number of fields = 41; mean number of fields per household = 2.9; mean number of individuals per household = 14.

Source: G. E. Currens, "Women, Men and Rice Organizational Innovations in Northwestern Liberia," Human Organization, vol. 35, no. 4, winter 1976, p. 361.

Table 7. Percentages of women in the economically active population by industry and country

Country	Year	Agriculture	Mining and Quarrying	Manufacturing	Construction	Electricity	Commerce	Transport	Services	Others
Algeria[1]	1966	1.8	1.8	8.8	0.5	3.8	2.5	2.6	15.3	3.0
Botswana	1971	20.8	4.4	5.9	2.5	-	22.8	-	18.7	-
Congo[1]	1967	-	-	2.5	0.3	0.2	6.6	1.0	13.8	-
Dahomey[1]	1967	18.1	-	-	-	-	95.0	-	10.2	-
Ethiopia[1]	1970	1.7	0.4	26.3	0.7	3.4	13.7	14.0	23.0	-
Egypt	1966	3.9	2.5	4.6	0.8	1.9	6.3	2.1	18.6	33.0
Gabon	1963	50.6	1.5	12.2	3.0	11.1	30.1	3.5	34.2	35.7
Ghana[1]	1970	57.2	1.0	12.0	2.3	-	13.9	2.9	10.5	-
Kenya[2]	1971	17.2	2.4	6.4	2.8	2.4	10.4	5.7	19.7	-
Liberia	1962	41.6	2.5	8.7	1.4	3.7	34.1	2.4	14.8	21.2
Libya[1]	1964	2.1	0.4	29.3	0.5	1.3	0.8	0.4	5.9	8.4
Madagascar[1]	1964	14.9	20.3	15.3	1.2	4.2	15.7	1.7	-	-
Malawi	1968	11.5	0.8	3.4	0.1	1.4	5.6	1.7	-	-
Mauritius[1]	1970	27.3	27.9	-	0.6	4.4	16.5	1.5	-	-
Morocco	1971	10.6	4.2	27.3	2.1	11.3	6.0	4.4	29.5	25.6
Niger	1960	10.3	-	-	-	-	9.4	-	17.3	-
Nigeria[1]	1965	9.9	2.0	4.8	0.3	1.0	5.7	2.4	12.9	-
Rwanda[1]	1969	1.1	0.2	3.2	-	-	-	-	-	-
Sierra Leone	1963	42.3	0.8	14.8	1.1	3.5	41.9	2.3	15.8	8.0
Tanzania-Main.	1967	51.1	1.9	9.9	0.7	2.7	9.4	1.5	18.8	-
Zanzibar	1967	53.0	-	55.7	3.6	0.2	13.9	2.6	14.7	18.2
Tunisia	1966	1.8	0.7	23.4	0.5	1.3	2.9	2.9	10.3	5.0
Uganda[1]	1969	1.8	-	3.4	0.3	-	6.4	1.5	-	-
Zambia	1969	12.2	4.3	7.5	2.5	-	-	3.5	-	-

Source: Year Book of Labour Statistics, ILO, Geneva, 1974.
1 UNECA Country Reports.
2 Employment and Earnings in the Modern Sector, 1971, General Bureau of Statistics: Ministry of Finance and Planning, 1973, Nairobi, Kenya.

Table 8

Comparative Wages in Agriculture and Manufacturing

Employ-ment	Country	Year	% of male salary earned by females	Year	% of women among workers in the category
Agri-culture	Ghana	1962	74	1962	4
		1970	79	1969	12
	Kenya	1962	34	1963	19
		1966	60	1966	18
	Morocco	1962	75	n/a	n/a
		1972	80		
Manu-factur-ing	Egypt	1962	53	n/a	n/a
		1967	67	1966	5
	Kenya	1962	74	1963	19
		1966	93	1966	18

Source: Yearbook of Labour Statistics.

Table 9

UNICEF Budget for Women's Group Programmes

(All in U.S. Dollars)

	1973	Budgeted 1974	1975	Total 73/75	Actually Expended	Un- expended
Transport, Supply & Equipment for trained women's group	-	3,900	-	11,700	-	11,700
Field super- visors (1 landrover)	-	4,000	-	4,000	-	4,000
Non-supply Women's leaders basic course	500	20,000	5,400	25,900	3,882	22,018
Seminars & conferences	2,600	20,000	17,900	40,500	4,402	36,098
Community De- velopment As- sistants & Youth Leaders Course	7,300	-	-	7,300	7,300	-
	10,400	47,900	31,100	89,400	15,584	73,816
Freight	-	500	-	500		
Total	10,400	48,400	31,100	89,900		

Table 10

UNICEF Budget for Support of Day Care Centres

(All in U.S. Dollars)

	1973	1974	1975	Total	Amount Disbursed	Balance
Transport supplies & equipment for teachers and supervisors	1,700	1,400	1,500	4,600	15,085	3,015
Model day care centre	5,700	7,200	8,600	21,500	5,400	16,100
Bicycles for supervisors	900	-	-	900	-	900
Teacher training	23,600*	13,900	13,900	51,400	will be spent in 1975	will be none
Evaluation staff workshop	1,400	1,400	1,500	4,300	1,300	3,000
Supervisors' training	9,700	7,700	7,700	25,100	1,705	23,295

*Includes estimate for 1972.